WITHDRAWN

The Desktop Designer's Illustration Handbook

The Desktop Designer's Illustration Handbook

Marcelle Lapow Toor

CORNELL UNIVERSITY

VAN NOSTRAND REINHOLD
I(T)P® A Division of International Thomson Publishing Company Inc.

New York • Albany • Bonn • Boston • Detroit • London • Madrid • Melbourne
Mexico City • Paris • San Francisco • Singapore • Tokyo • Toronto

Cover illustrations:
© Andrew Singer
© Ron Blalock
© Diana Bryan
Cover design: Paul Costello

Van Nostrand Reinhold Staff
Editor: Jane Degenhardt
Production Editor: Carla Nessler
Production Manager: Mary McCartney
Designer: Marcelle Lapow Toor

Copyright © 1996 by Van Nostrand Reinhold
I(T)P®   A division of International Thomson Publishing Inc.
The ITP logo is a registered trademark under license

Printed in the United States of America
For more information, contact:

Van Nostrand Reinhold
115 Fifth Avenue
New York, New York 10003

Chapman & Hall
2-6 Boundary Row
London
SE 8HN
United Kingdom

Thomas Nelson Australia
102 Dodds Street
South Melbourne 3205
Victoria, Australia

Nelson Canada
1120 Birchmount Road
Scarborough, Ontario
MIK 5G4, Canada

Chapman & Hall BmgH
Pappelallee 3
69469 Weinheim
Germany

International Thomson Publishing Asia
221 Henderson Road #05-10
Henderson Building
Singapore 0315

International Thomson Publishing Japan
Hirakawacho Kyowa Building, 3F
2-2-1 Hirakawacho
Chiyoda-ku, 102 Tokyo
Japan

International Thomson Editores
Seneca 53
Col. Polanco
11560 Mexico D.F. Mexico

1 2 3 4 5 6 7 8 9 10 BBR 02 01 00 98 97 96

Library of Congress Cataloging-in-Publication Data

Toor, Marcelle Lapow.
   The Desktop Designer's Illustration Handbook
   / Marcelle Lapow Toor
      p. 176   cm.

   Includes index.
   ISBN 0-442-02028-7
   1. Computer graphics—Handbooks, manuals, etc.
   2. Desktop publishing. I. Title
T385.T66   1996
741.6–dc20

95-51689
CIP

This book is dedicated to Rachel, Mark, and George

Acknowledgments

Many people were involved in the task of putting this book together. I want to thank my children, Rachel and Mark, for their support and enthusiasm. I could not have produced this book without the aid of my partner and mate, George Rhoads, who drew the playful illustrations for several of the chapter openers and assumed responsibility for many of the household tasks. My thanks and gratitude go to Nancy Jacobs, Antonia Demas, and Robin Remick, who read through the early chapters and gave me feedback and encouraging words, and the reviewers who reviewed the early manuscript for offering suggestions that helped solidify my ideas.

Steven Heller gave me helpful advice and provided me with names of some of the illustrators whose work appears in the book. Illustrator, Diana Bryan, helpful as always, recommended a number of fine illustrators who are represented here. Thanks to the many fine illustrators who contributed their work.

Many clip art and font software publishers provided me with copies of their software. They are represented in the sampler of digital clip art and fonts. I want to thank Good Impressions for sending me a huge assortment of their wonderful rubber stamps.

Finally, I am grateful to the staff at VNR—especially my editor, Jane Degenhardt, for all her help and understanding; Carla Nessler, who led me patiently through the production process; and Cynthia Biron, who listened to my marketing ideas.

Contents

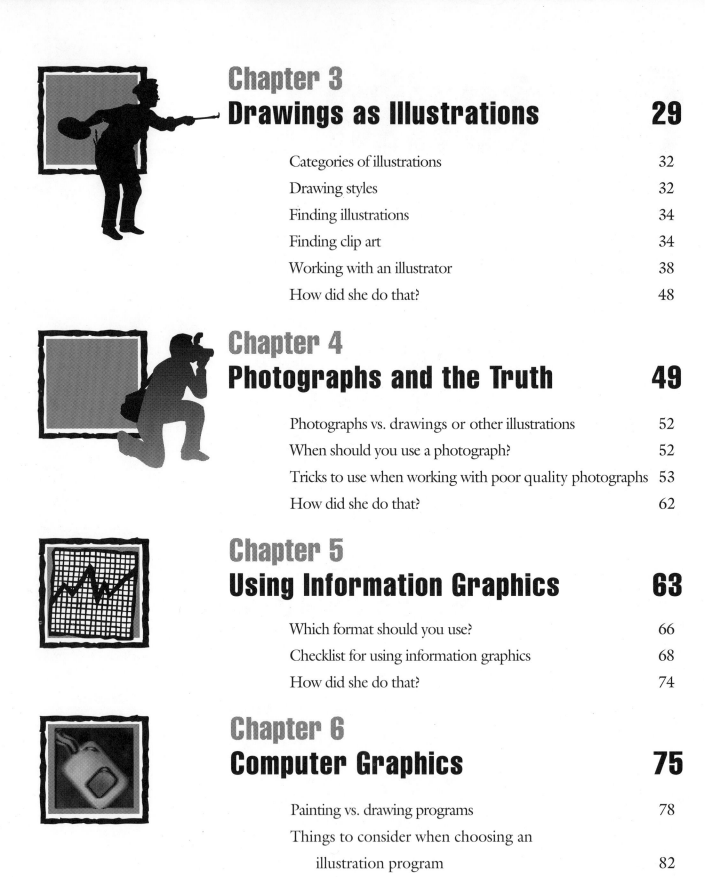

Introduction
Getting Noticed

Storefront in New York City.
Photographer: Harry Lapow, 1980
© Marcelle Lapow Toor

Chapter opener: The body with the radio is clip art. It has been combined
with musical notes and a face that were drawn by hand and scanned into Photoshop.

Getting Noticed

"We learn language by applying words to visual experiences,
and we create visual images to illustrate verbal ideas.
This interaction of word and image is the background
for contemporary communication."

—Allen Hurlburt, *The Design Concept.* 1989.

In the days before the Industrial Revolution, a familiar street sound was the singsong voice of the itinerant peddler who traveled from town to town selling a variety of wares from trinkets to food. The prospective buyer was able to examine the goods and handle them before making a purchase.

Today everything is packaged. The advertising industry has replaced the weather-beaten street vendor with his melodious voice. Products and printed materials in the form of ads, flyers, brochures, posters, magazines, and newspapers call out to us discordantly, each in competition for our attention.

We live in an information age where visual images accost us daily. The tools of communication surround us—graffiti on walls and public transportation, posters and flyers on bulletin boards, newspapers, magazines, movies, messages in the sky, and on our computers. We live in the midst of a media battle zone. To protect ourselves we have become quite sophisticated and very discriminating about the information we choose to absorb and the information we choose to tune out. Given this climate and your project, the design of a newsletter, or brochure, what can you do to get your printed piece noticed?

This book is for you if..

This book is for you if you are looking for help in creating more visually-exciting publications—printed pieces that make an impression and are noticed. This book is for you if you are a novice designer, desktop publisher, graphic design student, seasoned designer, or a student who wants to hand in a paper that is sure to get an A. It can be used as a guide and a resource in the selection and use of illustrations—illustrations that are ready-made, illustrations created by hired hands, or illustrations you create yourself that can be integrated with text on the page you are designing.

About this book ....

In order for a design to be successful—one that communicates visually—the designer must grab the audience with a visual attack. How do you do that? How do you reach jaded audiences suffering from visual overload? How can you use graphic images that will get noticed amongst the chaos? When do you use drawings in a publication? When is it more appropriate to use photographs? How can you use type as an illustration? How do you convey statistical information visually so that it is easily absorbed and understandable on first glance? What do you do when you are on a tight budget and can't afford illustrations? Where can you go to find that special illustration? This book is intended to provide answers to these questions to help you create designs with visual power.

Each chapter in this book contains illustrations, quotes, hints, and tips. This book showcases clip art, and decorative and pictorial fonts available on disk and CD-ROM, as well as addresses of the software manufacturers. A list of public and private image sources is included to help you in the search for that special picture.

Chapter 1 Creating a Visual Package

When you design a publication you are creating a visual package. The text is in place for your newsletter, but what kind of illustration(s) do you need to make it less deadly-looking, less gray, less monotonous? How do you make a decision about the kind of illustration to use for your newsletter or brochure? What are the choices? What questions do you need to ask before making a decision? This chapter discusses different kinds of illustrations as well as a list of questions for you to ask to help you decide which to use.

Chapter 2 Type and Graphic Devices

You have a nonexistent budget for your brochure. You can't draw, and can't afford to hire an illustrator or a photographer. Even clip art is beyond your budget. With all these strikes against you what can you do to give your printed piece some visual interest so it will not only attract attention but be attractive? Or, let's try another scenario. You have a reasonable budget but your newsletter is packed with text. There is no room on the page for a graphic, any graphic. What kind of cosmetic changes can you make to your pages to make your publication more interesting, less boring—enticing to your reader? The answer is type and typographic devices. This chapter discusses how type and typographic devices can be used to create graphic interest on a page—simple techniques to dress up your design and keep you within your budget and context of your publication.

Chapter 3 Drawings as Illustrations

You have decided that a drawing is the kind of illustration you need for your publication. What style of drawing is the one most appropriate for your printed piece? Where can you go to find the drawing you are looking for? Where can you find ready-made images to use in your publications? How can you find an illustrator to create that special illustration? This chapter discusses the many possibilities of using and finding drawings.

Chapter 4 Photographs and the Truth

It is a common belief that photographs represent the truth. People believe photographs more than drawings. When is it appropriate to use a photograph in a publication? When should you use a photograph rather than a drawing? What questions do you need to ask before making a decision to use a photograph? What can you do with a scanner to alter photographic images to achieve the effect or feel you want? If you decide that a photograph is the right kind of illustration for your publication, and you are not a photographer, where can you go to find photographs that will illustrate your publication and not drain your budget? This chapter discusses what to look for in a photograph, how to crop photographs for greater impact, and tricks to use when working with a poor-quality photograph.

Chapter 5 Using Information Graphics

Information graphics are being used a great deal these days. We are used to seeing illustrative charts and graphs in *USA Today*. How can you present statistical information in a visual way so your reader will understand and comprehend the information easily on first glance? When should you use a chart, graph, diagram, or table? This chapter examines the use of charts, graphs, tables, and maps as illustrative, visual devices when presenting data. It discusses how to select an appropriate format for presenting data in a way that is visually interesting. At the end of this chapter you will find a checklist for using charts and graphs successfully.

Chapter 6 Computer Graphics

Many illustrations are being rendered directly on the computer with drawing and painting programs. This chapter discusses the basic differences between these two programs, and the advantages and disadvantages of each. It contains illustrations done by professional illustrators with information on the programs and techniques used.

In this chapter you will see how a simple publication can be dressed up with a background texture created on the computer—an inexpensive way to take away the monotonous or vanilla look, and how a scanner and an image-editing program can be used to create textured backgrounds with a variety of readily available materials placed randomly on the scanner.

Chapter 7 Picture Sources

You have designed a brochure or a flyer that has an "old world" look. You need several illustrations to achieve that effect—ones that will reinforce that look and give your publication the feel you want. Where can you find the appropriate illustration? This chapter contains a list of picture resources in public and private collections that are available to the general public.

And there is more ....

- A list of the graphic devices used in each chapter with an explanation of how each was done
- Relevant quotes from graphic designers and illustrators
- Helpful tips and hints
- A sampler of clip art available on disk and CD-ROM
- A sampler of pictorial and decorative typefaces
- Illustrations from professional illustrators

ℯ ℯ ℯ ℯ ℯ

The right picture or graphic device will enhance your newsletter, brochure, flyer, or invitation, and attract the attention of your reader. Illustrations can add humor, a sense of realism, fancy or fantasy, sophistication or drama to any publication.

The newsletter graphic is from Image Club Graphics Woodcut series.

How did she do that?

A list of the graphic devices used in this chapter and how each was created

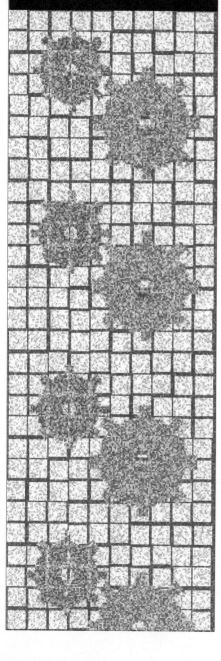

1.

Old Dreadful No. 7 by Bitstream was used for the drop cap on the first page of this chapter.

2.

This decoration comes from the font, Type Embellishments One from Letraset.

3.

This decoration is from the font, DF Mo Funky Fresh Symbols from Fontek.

4.

The column on the left was created by placing the gear graphic from page xiii into Photoshop and using the tile and noise filters.

Chapter 1
Creating a Visual Package

Illustration created as a self promotion for *American Showcase Directory of Illustrators*, 1994.
Illustrator: Leslie Cober-Gentry, Trumbull, CT

Chapter opener: The box is clip art from T/Maker's ClickArt Series.
The images inside the box are a combination of fonts and clip art.

Creating a Visual Package

"Visual language is already dominating verbal or at least written communication. If you think about it we've been growing up with a major change toward the visual, and computers have accelerated that change."
—John Waters, *Print* magazine. September/October 1993.

ou have come up with a design for your newsletter. It looks deadly. It's monotonous. It lacks color and graphic interest. It needs some pizzaz. You are in a panic. Your budget is nonexistent. You can't even afford to have the piece printed professionally. It will be reproduced on a copy machine. What kind of cosmetic changes can be made to dress it up, to make it look appealing and colorful even though you can only use one color? How can you create visual interest on the cover and inside pages so the person who receives the newsletter doesn't toss it into the trash without giving it a second glance? You need to turn your newsletter, brochure, flyer, poster, or magazine into a visual package—a successful marriage of illustrations and text.

Communication does not take place with text alone. Words do not have the same impact as pictures. "A picture is worth more than a thousand words," is an expression familiar to all of us and has even more meaning in today's world. The addition of good graphics will help enhance any printed piece. A good picture by itself will communicate. One that is well integrated with text can provoke an emotional response, make an impression, and help direct the reader through the layout of a page.

Visual images surround us in our daily lives. We see pictorial symbols in our homes on our microwave ovens, refrigerators, and answering machines. In our cars they inform and warn us when we are running low on gasoline or oil. Pictorial symbols are found on road signs. They speak a universal wordless language and make it easy for you to drive your car in a foreign country without knowing the language because they give you the information you need—deer crossings, sharp curves in the road. Graphic symbols are found in airports where people from many different countries convene. They identify telephones, restrooms, restaurants, smoking and non-smoking areas. Symbols in the form of simple graphics speak a visual universal language and help us find information quickly.

The graphic or graphics you select for your printed piece should be a vital element in your brochure, newsletter, or flyer. A brochure that lacks an illustration must have a very powerful verbal message in order to make an impression. Pictures or graphic images attract attention. They can add a sense of reality to a publication, establish a mood, involve our emotions, and may even entertain in the process. Some events are better described with a picture than with words.

The choice of a graphic image is directly related to the audience, the printed piece, and the kind of message to be communicated. The quality of the image has the same importance as its appropriateness. The illustration you use should be an integral element and one of the main pieces that fits into the overall layout.

Graphics in a publication should:

- Clarify the text
- Lead the reader through the text
- Attract attention
- Add a sense of realism
- Add a sense of fantasy
- Establish a mood
- Involve the emotions
- Entertain or explain

The best advice for using graphics is: keep it simple. A graphic should be easy to read and should be helpful in conveying important information. Research shows that photographs and other graphic images are used by readers as entry points onto a printed page. If the graphic you have selected does not contain information related to the text in your publication, leave it out and find another way to enhance the pages visually.

SELECTING ILLUSTRATIONS TO ENHANCE YOUR PAGE LAYOUT
Making decisions

Before making a decision about the kind of illustration you need for the printed piece you are designing, you may want to consider the following questions:

 1. Who is your audience?

Identify your audience. What kind of person do you want to reach? Is this audience a specific age, gender, or income level?

 2. What is the content of the message?

What do you want to say to this audience? What is the tone you want to set? Is it serious or do you want it to have humor?

 3. Will an illustration enhance your page design?

Can you find an appropriate illustration that will make your newsletter or brochure look more interesting and easier to read?

 4. What kind of art will attract your audience to help them absorb the textual information?

Do some research to find out what kind of art appeals to your intended audience—what kinds of images they identify with. A good place to start is your local newsstand. Look at current magazines that appeal to your audience. A cartoon-like drawing may be the best way to get the attention of kids because kids like cartoons and most of them watch TV. However, if the audience

The cartoon is clip art from T/Maker.

for your publication is the young professional, the sophisticated twenty-something crowd, the generation who watches *Melrose Place* on Monday nights, or the thirty-something crowd, fans of Northern Exposure, a photograph will attract better than a drawing.

5. What type of illustration should you use?

If you are designing a magazine spread for a short story for example, a drawing or painting (oil or watercolor) may have a better "feel" than a photograph, since a story is based on fiction. On the other hand, if you are designing a brochure for a human services organization, photographs of actual people would be more effective. If you have to explain complex statistical information, a chart, table, graph, or bulleted list would be a better choice. If you are unable to find a picture that seems just right, you can always do some interesting things with type and typographic devices.

6. Will the graphic attract attention?

Find a graphic that will be appropriate to your printed piece and appeal to your audience using an image that is both familiar and pleasant. The picture you choose should attract attention but not detract from the editorial content of your printed piece. It should enhance the text and act as a guide to help move the reader through the information on the page.

7. What kind of graphic image will reproduce well, given the printing process you will be using?

If you are producing the entire publication on the computer for reproduction on a photocopy machine, you are limited in the kinds of illustrations you can use. Photographs reproduced on a copy machine, even one equipped to copy photographs, will not appear as sharp as when a professional printer creates a screened halftone. Simple line drawings and clip art, however,

Above: Images from the pictorial font DF Naturals from Fontek.

will reproduce quite well when photocopied from a laser print out. Your budget will influence the choice you make.

 8. Who will create the graphic?

If you cannot draw and have a decent budget you may want to hire an illustrator or photographer. If you are on a tight budget, stock art or clip art that comes on disk, CD-ROM, or books might be the best solution.

WHAT ARE YOUR CHOICES?

All illustrations fit into two categories—line art and continuous tone art.

1. Type and Typographic Devices

When you are on a tight budget, type and typographic devices can be used very effectively as a means of illuminating text in a printed piece. Typographic devices include: dingbats, bullets, lines or rules, symbols, typographic ornaments, geometric shapes, large initial capital letters, patterned boxes, dots, and flags.

The painter and photographer are clip art images from Image Club Graphics. The photographer image was altered slightly with a gradual fill in FreeHand in order to represent the continuous tones found in photographs.

2. Drawings

Drawings fit into the category of line art. When we refer to drawings, we are talking about pictures rendered with pen and ink, paint or pencil. If you can't draw, don't. A poorly-executed drawing will make a potentially good publication scream, "amateur." Hire an illustrator if your budget will permit, or use clip art instead. Seasoned graphic designers use clip art when they need instant art. Clip art is available in many drawing styles, some quite sophisticated, and can be found on disks, CD-ROM, and in books.

3. Photographs

A photograph is made up of many gray tones, all the tones going from black to white, and falls into the

TIP 1:
It is better to use no art than art that is weak or poorly executed.

TIP 2:
Allow plenty of time for the creation of your illustration whether you do it yourself or hire an illustrator.

TIP 3:
Stick with a consistent art style throughout your publication.

TIP 4:
Use your illustrations as a means of guiding the reader through the text.

TIP 5:
Use graphics that relate to your printed piece, your message, and have ones that have some familiarity for your audience.

category of continuous tone art. Photographs are appropriate images to use when you want to document a real event or show actual people.

4. **Information Graphics**

Information graphics include: charts, graphs, diagrams, maps, and tables. An information graphic is a good way to present statistical information visually so that it is understandable. There are a number of software programs on the market that make it easy for you to create your own charts and graphs.

5. **Computer Generated Graphics**

The computer is replacing traditional drawing and painting tools for some illustrators. Many illustrators are using various painting and drawing programs to render complex illustrations.

QUESTIONS TO ASK BEFORE SELECTING A GRAPHIC

Is this the right type of illustration for my publication?

Is this illustration appropriate for my audience and the message?

Does the illustration tell a visual story related to the text?

Will this graphic enhance the page layout and lead the reader through the textual information on the page?

Will the size of the graphic help create a dramatic effect, or will it get lost on the page?

Is the image unambiguous so that my readers will understand it immediately?

Does the graphic have a credit line or caption as a means of identifying what it is and who created it?

Woman at the Easter Parade, NYC, 1980.
Photographer: Harry Lapow
© Marcelle Lapow Toor

Illustrations will:

1. **Attract attention**

   Readers will stop to read an illustration.

2. **Provide a place for the reader's eyes to rest**

   Illustrations will provide relief from a page full of text.

3. **Help an audience remember your printed piece**

   Strong images make a lasting impression.

4. **Establish an ambiance for your publication**

   An illustration will help to reinforce the setting—the look and feel of your newsletter or brochure.

5. **Help the reader comprehend complex information**

   Illustrations can lead the reader through the written text and explain information in a visual way.

 Keep a swipe file (examples of images from magazines and other publications) with illustrations that appeal to you. These samples can help with ideas when you are working with an illustrator or creating your own drawings.

 A good slogan to remember when using graphics is, "keep it simple."

The chapters that follow cover each type of illustration (type, drawings, photographs, information graphics, and computer generated graphics) in greater detail.

How did she do that?

A list of the graphic devices used in this chapter and how each was created

1.

The number and the initial capital letter on the first page of this chapter are from the Letraset font, Zinzaro. The Y was converted to paths in FreeHand and filled with a graduated fill.

2.  **?**

A question mark from the Adobe typeface, Aachen Bold, was converted to paths in FreeHand. The circle on the bottom was replaced with a rectangle.

3.

This bird is from a font called, DF Mo Funky Fresh Symbols, from Fontek.

4.

The column on the left was created by putting clip art from Image Club Graphics into Photoshop and using the difference cloud filter.

Chapter 2
Type and Graphic Devices

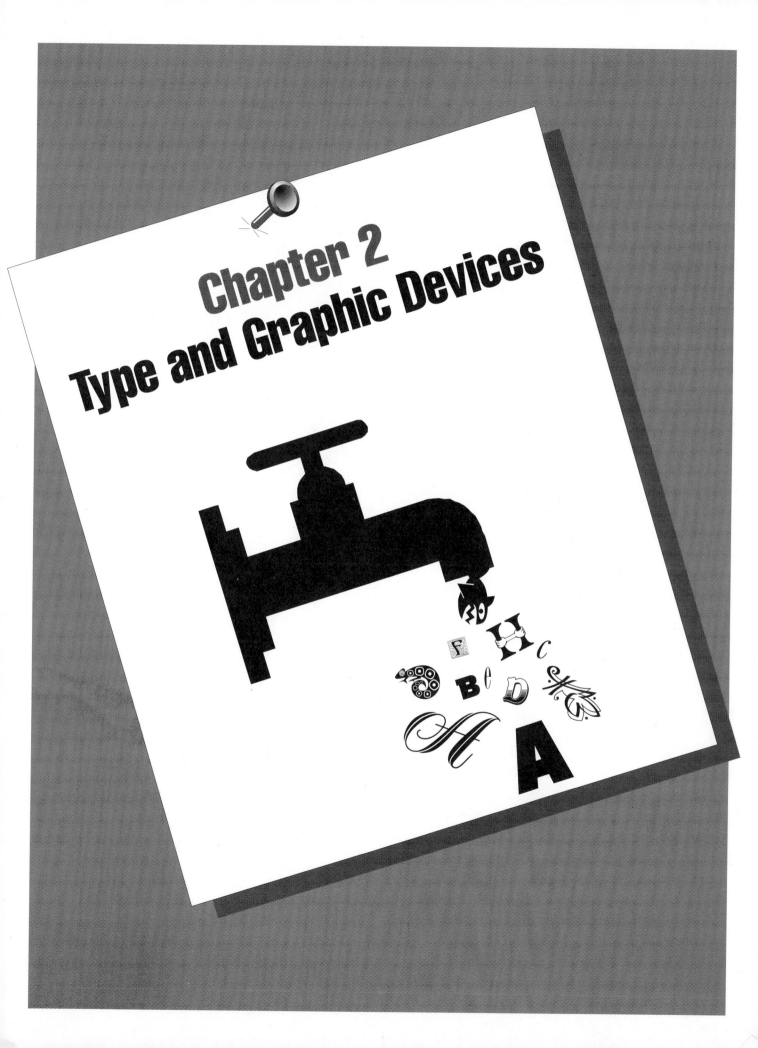

Call for entries for the Type Directors Club annual competition.
Designer/illustrator: Daniel Pelavin

Chapter opener: The faucet is clip art from T'Maker's Click Art Series.
It was altered in FreeHand. The fonts were added in PageMaker.

2

Type and Graphic Devices

"Type is a thing of constant interest... It is sometimes
a serious and useful tool, employed to deliver a message,
sell a specific article, or give life to an idea."
—Bradbury Thompson.

e are all used to seeing type on a page. We are so accustomed to seeing type as text that when we are designing a page we don't see it or think of its potential as a graphic element on a page. We only look at it in terms of words.

If you are on a tight budget or are producing a publication like a newsletter that has a great deal of text with no room for any kind of illustration (drawings, photographs, charts, and graphs), how are you going to dress up your printed piece and make it visually interesting so that it will grab your audience? The answer is type and typographic devices. Let type act as a visual medium. Type can be used as a graphic to communicate visually. An attack with type can be a good strategy when you can't afford illustrations or do not have space to include pictures. Type used well can be an effective communication tool. It can be used to illustrate words, provide color, and create contrast on a black-and-white page.

You do not need a large budget to make your layout graphically interesting. Type and typographic devices provide numerous options for decorating a page and enhancing a design. This chapter discusses how to use type as a visual, and provides examples of type and graphic devices that can be used for illustration.

USING TYPE AS ILLUSTRATION

What are the options?

- Drop caps, raised caps, and caps in boxes
- Shaped text
- Enlarged numbers
- Enlarged punctuation marks
- Ampersands
- Typographic ornaments
- Dingbats
- Pull quotes or call outs
- Lines/rules, dots, checks, and stripes
- Graphic devices
- Patterns
- Boxes or borders

❖ **Drop caps, raised caps, and caps in boxes**

A drop cap is a large initial capital letter that fits neatly and "drops" into a paragraph. Drop caps can be set into boxes like the one on the first page of this chapter and several other chapters in this book.

A large intial capital letter does not have to drop into the paragraph. It can sit on the first line of text in a paragraph and rise above the paragraph.

Large initial capital letters

Drop cap

Lorem ipsum dolor sit amet, ut wisi consectetuer sed diam nonummy nibh euism. Od tincidunt laoreet dolore magna aliquam erat volut. Ut wisi enim ad minim veniam, quis nostrud cor exercitation ullam suscipit lobortis nisl ut aliquip ex ea commodo consequat. Duis autem vel eum iriure dolor in hendrerit in. Ut wisi enim ad minim veniam, quis exercitation. Consequat, vel illum dolore.

Drop cap reversed in a box

Lorem ipsum dolor sit amet, ut wisi consectetuer sed diam nonummy nibh euism tincidunt laoreet dolore magna aliquam erat volut. Ut wisi enim ad minim veniam, quis nostrud cor exercitation ullam suscipit lobortis nisl ut aliquip ex ea commodo consequat. Duis autem vel eum iriure dolor in hendrerit in. Ut wisi enim ad minim veniam, quis nostrud exercitation aliquam erat.

Raised cap

Lorem ipsum dolor sit amet, ut wisi consectetuer sed diam nonummy nibh euismd tinci ismdunt laoreet dolore magna aliquam erat volut. Ut wisi enim ad minim veniam, quis nostrud cor exerci tation ullam suscipit lobortis nisl ut aliquip ex ea commodo consequat. Duis autem vel eum iriure dolor in hendrerit in. Ut wisi enim ad minim veniam, quis nostrud exercitation.

❖ Shaped text

It is possible to create text that conforms to a shape by using the text wrap or runaround function in your page layout program. Shaped text can also be created in a drawing program.

❖ Enlarged numbers

Large numbers, ones that are larger than the point size of the body text, can be used to create visual interest and draw the reader's attention to information on a page.

❖ Enlarged punctuation marks

Exclamation marks, question marks, commas, and quotation marks that are oversized can provide graphic interest on a page.

❖ Ampersands

The ampersand, the symbol for 'and' (&), can be used as a graphic. The ampersand symbol, an interesting shape in itself, exists in each typeface. The shapes differ depending on the typeface you select.

❖ Typographic ornaments

Typographic ornaments are decorative devices in the form of curlicues, flourishes, and brackets and can be found in fonts or clip art (see appendix 2, Sampler of Specialty Fonts).

❖ Dingbats

Dingbats are decorative devices, graphic symbols, that can be used as bullets when listing items that do not follow an order of importance. The bullets on the left are from the font Zapf Dingbats from Adobe Systems, Inc.

❖ Pull quotes or call outs

Pull quotes and call outs are quotes from an article that are pulled out of the body copy of the text. They are used as a device to get the attention of the reader.

The fonts represented in the box above are, from top to bottom: Eras Demi, Bronx, Black Chancery, Greyton Script, Mistral, Old Dreadful, and Arriba Arriba.

❖ Lines/rules, dots, checks, and stripes

Lines or rules provide a means of dressing up a page that is heavy with text. Rules can be light or heavy depending on your design and the number of them that will appear on a page. The rules can be solid, dotted, created with symbols, or made out of a pictorial typeface. Used simply, rules can define or separate areas on a page and help lead the reader through the text on the page. Too many rules will confuse the reader and make the page look busy and uninviting.

❖ Graphic devices

Geometric shapes—rectangles, circles, triangles, stars, diamonds, squiggles, boxes, borders, checks, dots, and others—can be put on a page of your publication to create visual interest. If they interfere with the readability of your newsletter or brochure, do not use them. They should be used sparingly.

❖ Patterns

Lines of type or several words that are repeated will create a pattern and texture for a page that is visually uninteresting. Patterns can also be made up of one repeated letter.

❖ Boxes or borders

Important information can be separated from the body of text and put in box or within a border. The box or border will call attention to itself and tell the reader to pay attention to the information presented. Borders can be created in a drawing program or with decorative/pictorial fonts. They are also available as clip art.

This border was created with the Fontek font, DF Moderns.

Borders can be made out of clip art and the box tool in the toolbox of your page layout program.

This box on the right has been created using the rectangle tool in PageMaker, clip art from T/Maker, and the font Greyton Script.

You are cordially invited to attend a private concert of the Chamber Music Society of Central New York.

8:15 p.m.

Typographic ornaments

This border comes from clip art found in Adobe Persuasion. The lines can be made thicker, and it can be filled with a color, black, or a graduated fill.

This border was created using the font Type Embellishments One by Fontek.

The decorative element on the top of this box, Flourish 3, is clip art from Image Club Graphics.

This border, called Ornate Plaque, is clip art from Past Tints.

Shaped text or text on a path

Text can be shaped in a drawing program to conform to a special shape or object. The quote from *Alice in Wonderland* on the right was typeset in FreeHand. A question mark was typed separately and converted to paths. The command "bind to path" was used and the quote followed the line formed by the question mark.

Text wrap

The text below has been shaped using the text wrap function in PageMaker. It has been shaped to conform to the head in the clip art graphic from T/Maker.

Lorem ipsum dolor sit amet, consectetuer adipiscing elit, sed diam nonummy nibh euismod tincidunt ut laoreet dolore magna aliquam erat volutpat. Ut wisi enim ad minim veniam, quis nostrud exerci tation ullamcorper suscipit lobortis nisl ut aliquip ex ea commodo consequat. Duis autem vel eum iriure dolor in hendrerit in vulputate velit esse molestie consequat, vel illum dolore eu feugiat nulla facilisis at vero eros et accumsan et iusto odio dignissim qui blandit praesent luptatum zzril delenit augue duis dolore laoreet dolore magna aliquam erat volutpat.

The quote in the black box on the right is called a pull quote or call out. It is used to catch the attention of the reader.

olor sit amet, lorem ipsum consectetuer ametcon sectetuera dipiscing elit, sed diam nonum my nibh euismod tincidunt ut laoreet dolore magna aliquam erat volutpat. Ut wisi enim ad minim velobris veniam, lorem ipsum quis nostrud exercitation ullam corper suscipit lobortis nisl ut aliquip exea commodo consequat.

Dolor sit amet, lorem ipsum consectetuer ametcon erat sectetuer adipiscing elit, sed diam nonummy nibh erat euismod tincidunt ut laoreet

dolore magna aliquam erat volutpat ut wisi enim.

Duis autem vel eum dipiscing elit, sedimet magna

THIS IS A CALL OUT. IT IS A GOOD ATTENTION-GETTER IN A MAGAZINE OR NEWSLETTER.

ediam nonum iriu dolor in hendrerit in vulputate velit esse molestie consequat, vel illum dolore eu feugiat nulla. Lorem ipsum dolor sit amet, consect etuer adipiscing elit. Ut wisi enim ad minim veniam. Ut wisi enim adminim ut elobris.

Triangles have been used as a graphic device in the layout on the left to add color and visual interest to the overall design.

Simple graphic devices can make a boring page more interesting

olor sit amet, lorem ipsum consect ut diam etuerametcon sectetue dipscing elit, sed diam nonum my nibh euismod tincidunt ut laoreet dolore magna aliquam erat volutpat. Ut wisi enim ad minim velobris veniam, lorem ipsum quis nostrud exercitation ullam corper suscipit lobortis nisl ut aliquip exea commodo consequat.

Dolor sit amet, lorem ipsum consectetuer ametcon erat sectetuer adipiscing elit, sed diam nonummy nibh erat euismod tincidunt ut laoreet

dolore magna aliquam erat volutpat.

Duis autem vel eum dipiscing elit, sedimet magna aliq liamuamediam nonum. Iriu dolor in hendrerit init vulputate velit esse molestie consequat, vel illum dolore eu feugiat nulla. Lorem ipsum dolor sit amet, consectetuer adipiscing elit.

Ut wisi enim ad minim veniam. Ut wisi enim lad minim velobris veniam, lorem ipsum nulla elit dipcing quis nostrud exercitationullam etuer ametcon sit amet, lorem.

Punctuation marks as shapes

Some question marks, commas, exclamation marks, quotation marks, and the various symbols on the computer's keyboard have interesting shapes and can be used to provide visual emphasis on an otherwise boring page.

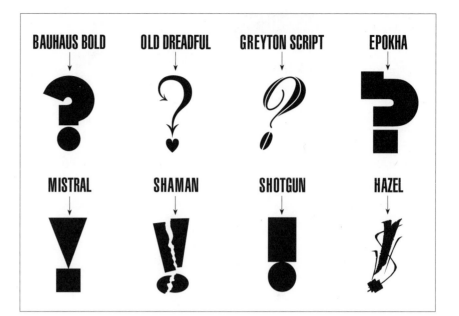

Special characters—Bodoni font

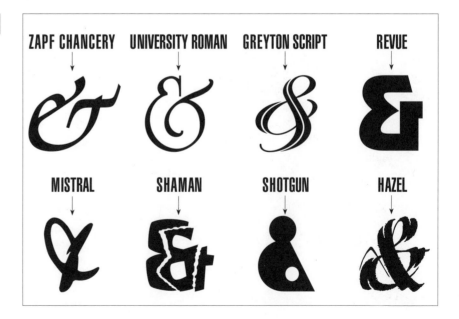

The ampersand as a shape

Dingbats

Dingbats are symbols that can be used as bullets or for decoration. The two dingbats on the right are clip art from T/Maker. The ones on the far right are from the font Zapf Dingbats.

Decorative initials from clip art

These decorative initials are clip art from Letraset.

Decorative initials from fonts

These decorative letters are from the Adobe font Ann Stone. They are good to use for large initial caps when you want an Art Deco look for your printed piece.

Tone types

These tone types are clip art from Letraset and can be altered in a drawing program to suit the needs of your publication. They can be used (in small amounts) for bullets, drop caps, or quotes.

Creating patterns with type

The example on the right shows type that has been grayed out, or ghosted. It acts as a pattern on the page. The example on the far right, shows lines of type that have been used to create a pattern and a feeling of movement. FreeHand was used for both designs.

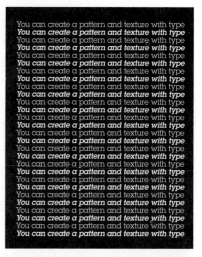

Patterns and special effects

This example shows a line of text, "What is graphic design?" that has been repeated and placed in Photoshop where the "difference clouds" and "extrude" filters were used.

Creating patterns with one letter

The repetition of one letter can create an intriguing pattern when negative space is involved. When the M's from the typeface Epokha are put together, arrows and rectangles appear in the negative space creating a pattern within a pattern.

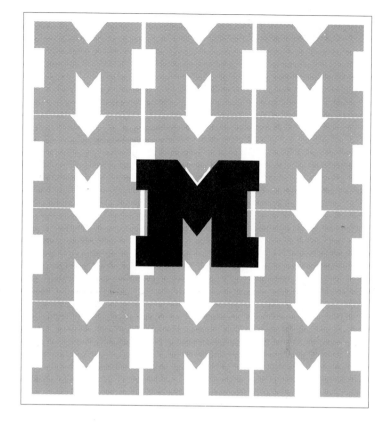

Creating a sense of movement with one letter

In this example, the calligraphic typeface, Bronx plain, was used in both upper and lowercase to create this freer texture. The italized typeface helps give an impression of movement.

The words that appear on this page demonstrate the meanings of the words.

Sandpaper, ripple, and pinch were created in Adobe Photoshop using the noise, ripple, and pinch filters.

The word, smile, was created using an envelope shape in the type manipulation program, LetraStudio by Letraset.

The words bite and dropout were created in FreeHand by converting the type to paths and altering each letter.

A logotype is a logo or symbol created with letters.

Top left: Logotype for Gazelle Inc., a sportswear company specializing in basketball apparel.
Designer: Doreen Caldera
Art directors: Doreen Caldera, Paul Caldera
Design firm: The Kottler Caldera Group

Top right: Logotype for Troxel Cycling and Fitness Inc., a manufacturer of cycling and fitness products.
Designer: Dave Kottler
Art directors: Paul Caldera, Dave Kottler, Doreen Caldera
Design firm: The Kottler Caldera Group

Left: Logotype for Art/Science Studio Lab, a custom photography lab and studio.
Designer: Marcelle Lapow Toor

Far right: Logotype for Backbone Design.
Designers: Steve Carsella, Chris Jones

Left: Logotype for Visitor Industry Plan for Greater Miami Convention and Visitor's Bureau
Art Director: Bruce Turkel
Designer: Sally Field
Design firm: Turkel Schwartz & Partners

Bottom left: Logotype for C&D, a plumbing company.
Designer: David R. Street
Design firm: Streetworks Studio

Bottom right: Logotype for Arsenal Publishing, Inc., a company that sells computer war game software and tactical manuals.
Design firm: Streetworks Studio

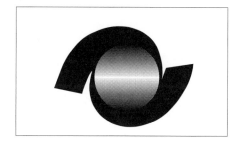

The page layouts on this page
show how text can be used as
an illustration. The text in each
example has been used to create
an object: a gear in the page
layout for the *Houston Chronicle*
(top) and part of a bicycle chain
in the design for the magazine,
AdNews (bottom).

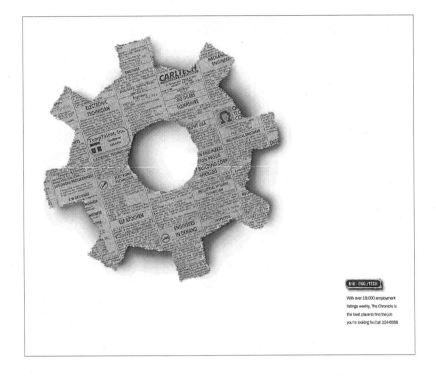

Ad for the *Houston Chronicle*
Art director: Jesus Felix
Creative director: Ray Redding
Copywriter: Cortny Jackson
Agency: Rives Carlberg

Ad for *AdNews* magazine
Designer: Richard Oliver
Photographer: Michael Schoenfield
Copywriter: Sara White
Agency: FJCandN

Illustration for Verbatum, a computer storage company.
Illustrator: Leslie Cober-Gentry

Cover for a catalog of stock illustrations. This design uses lines and geometric shapes as graphic devices.
Illustrator/designer: Daniel Pelavin

How did she do that?

A list of the graphic devices used in this chapter and how each was created

1.

The number two is from the Digital Typeface Corporation (DTC) typeface Vivante.

2.

The drop cap on the first page is from the DTC typeface Vivante.

3.

The column on the left was created in Adobe Photoshop using the Fontek font called Shaman, also shown above, and the wave filter.

Chapter 3
Drawings as Illustrations

1994 annual report for Bancorp, Today's Bancorp.
Designer: Scott Dvorak
Art director: Jeff Larson
Design firm: The Larson Group, Rockford, IL

Chapter opener: The painting is clip art from Past Tints Antique Illustrations.
It has been combined with a drawing. Illustrator: George Rhoads

Drawings as Illustrations

 he word "illustration" comes from the Latin word, "lustrare," meaning to make bright. The illustrator, Howard Pyle, in the early part of the 20th century, described illustration, "As every word is the cloak of a living thought, so the term "illustration" covers the idea of the bringing of a bright light." The purpose of an illustration, picture, graphic, or image is to clarify and interpret verbal information in a visual way—in other words—to illuminate.

When you contemplate a design for a newsletter, brochure, or other printed material you are thinking in terms of solving a specific problem for a specific audience. If you decide that a drawing is the right kind of illustration for your page layout, the drawing style and subject matter should be part of the solution to your problem as well.

A drawing, an image created with pen, pencil, or paint, has its own special appeal. It can speak to our sense of fancy and fantasy and stimulate our imaginations. Most people are fascinated by a well-executed picture. When a drawing shows a great deal of imagination and creativity, we take notice. If a drawing looks amateurish, it will make a well-designed publication scream, "amateur." It will attract attention for the wrong reason. A good drawing should attract attention and should be an integral part of the overall design.

You have made a decision to use a drawing or several drawings for your printed piece. What category of drawing do you need? What drawing style will best meet the needs of your printed piece and appeal to your audience? Where will you find the images you need?

CATEGORIES OF ILLUSTRATIONS

All illustrations fit into one of the categories listed below:

1. **Advertising**
2. **Editorial: magazines, newsletters, and newspapers**
3. **Fashion**
4. **Book**
5. **Medical and technical**
6. **Cartoons and caricatures**

DRAWING STYLES

Drawings fit into different styles.

1. **Line drawings**

   Line drawings refer to illustrations done in pen and ink, pencil, pastel, or crayon with either bold or delicate lines. Line art will hold up well under any reproduction process—photocopying or professional printing—and will reproduce well on most paper. Sophisticated and complex line drawings can be found in clip art on disk (see Appendix 1 for samples of available clip art).

2. **Woodcuts**

   Woodcuts are prints that are created by gouging out a drawing or design on a wooden block using a special tool. The design or image is cut with the grain, causing extra lines in the image. This is a good style to use when you want to show an artist's hand at work. (Appendix 1 has samples of stock art images that use this style.)

Top: Line art drawing from T/Maker's Studio Select clip art.

Bottom: This teapot and mug in woodcut style are from Image Club Graphics' Woodcut clip art.

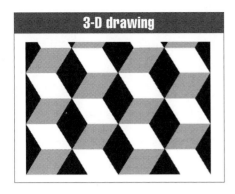

3-D drawing

This three-dimensional pattern is from Adobe Photoshop. PostScript patterns give an illusion of depth.

Silhouette

The rooster and pig use a silhouette style. They are from Image Club Graphics' Animal series.

Computer graphic

This logo was designed in FreeHand for a panel discussion at Cornell University sponsored by Women in Communication, "Women, Work, and Sex Discrimination: How Far Have We Come?" Illustrator: Marcelle Lapow Toor. 1993.

3. **Wet media (watercolor, oil)**

Professional illustrators often use watercolors, acrylics, or oil paints to create their illustrations. Sometimes, for special effects, an illustrator will use a wash, paint, or ink watered down and applied with a brush to get a soft and delicate effect or airbrush.

4. **Three-Dimensional drawings**

Architectural drawings and drawings of products need to show depth, making 3-D drawings essential as illustrations. Because of the illusion they create 3-D effects are fascinating.

5. **Silhouette**

In a silhouette, the entire drawing is filled in with one color. The silhouette emphasizes the shape of the drawing itself. Since the silhouette is an old art form it can be a way to inspire nostalgic feelings and take the reader back in time.

6. **Computer graphics**

The computer is a medium, not a style, a relatively new drawing tool for the illustrator. Simple and complex drawings can be created at your desktop with a drawing software program. Many illustrators have mastered these programs and are creating sophisticated and complex drawings. Illustrations created on the computer are easy to place on a page layout. Placing graphics on a page cuts cost because the printer does not need to take additional steps in the printing process. The work is camera-ready.

When using drawings for a printed piece you need to select an image(s) that will best enhance your text, complement your design, as well as appeal to your targeted audience. It is always better not to use any drawing than to use one that is amateurish, inappropriate, or misleading.

FINDING ILLUSTRATIONS

How do you find just the right image for your printed piece if you can't draw and do not have much of a budget? Where can you go to find finished art that will dress up your publication and not drain your financial resources? On the other hand, what if you have a large budget and want to hire someone to create illustrations just for your publication? What are your options and where can you go to find just the source you need?

The type of drawing you use is dependent upon your budget. There are a number of choices available.

Clip art from *Art Deco Spot Illustrations and Motifs, 513 Original Designs* by William Rowe. Dover Publications, 1985

1. Stock or clip art

Stock or clip art is finished art, either drawings or photographs, by artists and photographers using a number of different styles. By definition, clip art is art that is uncopyrighted, art that can be used without permission. Clip art was originally created for designers who were creating newspaper ads at the turn of the century and needed illustrations in a hurry. It is still used for that purpose, but with the arrival of the desktop computer its use is wider. If you need simple images and cannot draw, clip art provides a good means of illustrating your publications. Graphics on disk can enhance your publication and will reproduce well. The negative side of clip art is that it is available to the general public and many of the images have been overused. There is a good possibility that the images you select for your publication will have appeared in dozens of other publications as well. Overused images become stale quickly and are easily overlooked. But on a more positive note, clip art can be altered and customized to suit your needs and to get rid of the "canned" look.

FINDING CLIP ART

Clip art publications

A number of publishers specialize in producing books with ready-made art. Dover Publications is one of the largest publishers of clip art books that range from its

Pictorial Archive Series, a collection of images from archival materials, old drawings, engravings, and woodcuts, to books with more modern designs. Other publishing companies that publish clip art source books are: Art Direction Book Company, Hart Publishing, Sutphen Studio, and Graphic Products Corporation's North Light Books. The clip art in these books can be scanned or copied and pasted onto a finished page layout. The general rule for using clip art from these books is that you can use up to 10 images from one book without permission.

Clip art monthly services

Clip art can be purchased through a subscription service, a year's contract on a monthly basis like a magazine. The images may consist of art relating to the seasons, landscapes, portraits, sports, and food. Some companies that offer this service include: Metro Creative Graphics, Dynamic Graphics, PMS, and Stamp Conhaim. Some of the images are on disk and some on paper. Yearly subscriptions are payable monthly and prices range from $300 to $4,000 per year depending on the service you select. Most of these companies will provide you with a catalog to give you an idea of their graphic offerings.

Clip art on disk and CD-ROM

In the past, clip art was only available from books and subscription services. Now you can get clip art on disk and CD-ROM. Numerous software publishers have collections of clip art in different categories—animals, business, people, sports, food, medicine, technology, and recreation. The disks are relatively inexpensive and you can build a library with a variety of images in different styles to dress up and enhance your brochures, newsletters, invitations, or flyers (see appendix 1 for actual images from different software publishers).

This disk is clip art from T/Maker. It has been rotated in PageMaker.

2. Art in public domain: Old books, postcards, and posters

Public domain refers to uncopyrighted art or art where the copyright has expired.

Old books, postcards, and posters are excellent sources for illustrations. Antique or secondhand shops are good resources for old books, postcards, and posters. Many of the items sold are so old they are in public domain and copyright-free. If you are looking for a specific image, are on a tight budget, and can't find what you are looking for in clip art books or on disk, old books are a good resource (see chapter 7, Picture Sources). Your local librarian may be the person to help you to find the appropriate picture.

A note of caution

Illustrations that have appeared in old magazines or books may still be under copyright and you may need permission to use them. If you are in doubt about the status of the copyright, contact the publisher of the book or magazine to get permission.

3. Pictorial fonts

Many software companies that sell fonts have some fonts that are illustrative or pictorial. Zapf Dingbats by Adobe include little symbols that can be used as graphics (see appendix 2).

Top row: The creatures are from the Fontek font called DF Mo Funky Fresh Symbols.

Bottom row: The food images are from a font called MiniPic Little Edibles from Image Club Graphics.

The image of the rubber stamp is clip art from Image Club Graphics.

The three rubber stamps above from old drawings are from Good Impressions.

4. Art in public and private collections

(see chapter 7, Picture Sources)

5. Computer generated graphics

Simple and complex graphics can be created on the computer with the many drawing, illustration, and image-editing programs available. Many professional illustrators are using the computer as a tool (see chapter 6, Computer Graphics).

6. Rubber stamps

Rubber stamps are another source of illustrations. If you are designing a brochure or a flyer with a small print run, a rubber stamp with the appropriate image will enhance your design without great expense. The image can be hand-stamped on each of the flyers using different colored inks. You can turn an inexpensively produced black and white printed piece into a two or three color design.

A rubber stamp has a unique look and feel, and there are endless images to be found from a variety of rubber stamp manufacturers. Good Impressions, a company based in Shirley, WV, has a catalog of Victorian images from archival materials that have been turned into stamps. Rubber stamps can be purchased in craft shops, and art or office supply stores along with pads of varying colors. *Rubber Stamp Madness,* a newsletter produced in Oregon, is a publication that showcases rubber stamp images and has articles for stamp collectors.

7. Hiring an illustrator
Freelance illustrators

If you hire an illustrator you should be able to get the exact illustration you want. It is possible to find an illustrator within your budget. If you haven't purchased art before and don't know what fees you may have to pay, you should look at *The Pricing and Ethical Guidelines,* a book published by the Graphic Artist Guild. You need to find an illustrator whose style will match and complement the style of your printed piece. Finding the right illustrator will take some research.

This quilt design is Click Art from T/Maker.

WORKING WITH AN ILLUSTRATOR

You may have to interview many illustrators and look at numerous portfolios before making a decision about which one to hire. The best way to go about the process is to look through some of the design periodicals that showcase good design *(Print, Communication Arts,* or *How),* or *The Illustrators' Blackbook,* a book that showcases work by individual artists. Find illustrations and styles that appeal to you and contact the illustrator to find out about cost and availability.

The illustrator you choose is your employee. You must be able to communicate your ideas and oversee the process.

Tips on working with an illustrator

1. **Once you have selected an illustrator, ask for references from previous clients.**

   Make some telephone calls to find out about the illustrator's performance. Some artists are excellent at what they do but are unable to meet deadlines.

2. **Write up a contract that spells out the terms of your agreement.**

   The contract should specify a deadline for the final art, as well as deadlines for preliminary sketches.

3. **Ask for some simple preliminary sketches after your first encounter.**

   You want to make sure your illustrator is on track and the images are what you had in mind.

4. **Know in advance what you want from your illustrator, but be open and flexible to the illustrator's ideas.**

   A professional illustrator may have ideas that will lead to a better illustration than the one you originally had in mind.

5. **Keep a swipe file with examples of illustrations from magazines or books to show the illustrator styles and designs you like.**

   It's always a good idea to show your illustrator looks you like.

6. **Give the illustrator a copy of your page designs with the text to be illustrated.**

   Your illustrator will need to know the exact size of the space you have allotted for the illlustration.

7. **Set a reasonable deadline for the illustrations and make sure your illustrator is capable of meeting it.**

   Professional artists and designers are used to working on a tight schedule and should be able to meet a reasonable deadline.

Working with an illustrator is a collaborative activity. The illustrator is a member of your team. Exploring ideas and brainstorming is part of the fun and excitement in working with another artist.

〉〉〉〈〉 〉〉〉〈〉 〉〉〉〈〉

Following are illustrations rendered by professional illustrators to help you with ideas and inspiration.

Right: This face was created using the font Fatline Bold. The nose width was changed to 80% of the original and the mouth widened to 130%.

A rebus substitutes pictures or symbols for words.

The eye and the ear images in this rebus are clip art, from the Woodcut series, from Image Club Graphics. The U is from the font Futura Bold.

The I and U in this rebus are from the font called Old Dreadful, and the heart is clip art from Image Club Graphics.

Pictograms

Logos, icons, or pictograms, pictorial representations of an object, are used as universal symbols in public places, such as airports, to help travelers who speak different languages locate washrooms and telephones. You can create your own pictograms in a drawing or painting program using clip art or pictorial fonts.

This pictogram uses the pictorial font called MiniPicLil Critters. The circle with the slash was drawn in FreeHand.

Pictorial fonts as illustrations

The graphics in the designs on this page are pictorial fonts—fonts that use pictures instead of letters—from Fontek and Image Club Graphics. Images from the fonts serve as illustrations. Repeating the image creates a decorative pattern. The fonts are an inexpensive, and are quick and easy sources for spot illustrations.

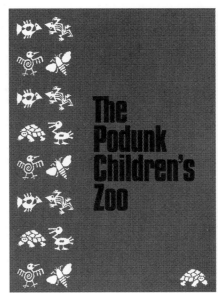

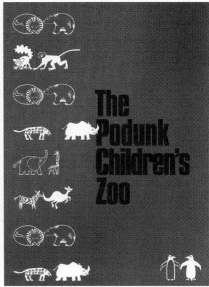

Left: DF Mo Funky Fresh Symbols, a font from Fontek, was used to create the pattern in the design for the Podunk Children's Zoo.

Right: MiniPicsLilCritters from Image Club Graphics was used to create the pattern in the design for the Podunk Children's Zoo.

Below left and right: Front and back covers for a booklet. The reptile images are from the font MiniPicsLilCritters.

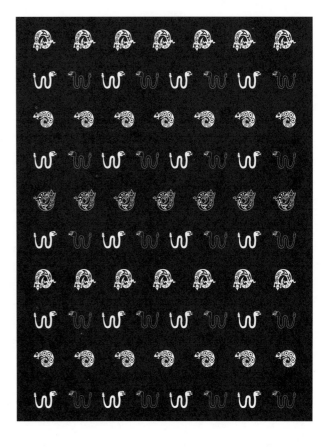

The illustrations on this page were created by Andrew Singer. In these cartoon-like drawings he has taken familiar expressions that lend themselves to visual translations.

DOG-EAT-DOG (THE CORPORATE YIN-YANG)

A HOLDING PATTERN...

BREAK FREE OF T.V.

" ENTERTAINING A THOUGHT "

Andrew Singer
P.O. Box 14392
Berkeley, CA 94712
Phone: 617. 789.4759

"I work in many media: gouache, watercolor, pencil, and colored pencil and pen and ink. I try to use light-fast India ink and an inexpensive but good quality acid-free paper. I often make small corrections with a brush and a jar of Pro-white—an opaque white watercolor."

Andrew Singer cartoons and illustrations have appeared in *The New Yorker, Discover, Adbusters, Z Magazine, The Progressive, The Monthly,* and other publications.

Top right: Self-portrait.

Bottom left: Illustration for an article for *Z Magazine* about the danger of exporting pesticides.

Bottom right: Illustration for *The Daily Californian* to show the imbalance between research and teaching in the academic world.

Diana Bryan

PO Box 391
Saugerties, NY 12477
Phone: 914. 246.3182

Diana Bryan, an illustrator, lecturer, and author, is also an award winning animator. Her client list includes, *The New York Times*, American Express, IBM, *Rolling Stone*, *Sports Illustrated*, and *The Wall Street Journal*. Diana Bryan's paper cutouts have been exhibited in galleries and are in the permanent collection of the Smithsonian Institute and the Library of Congress. She is a faculty member of Parsons School of Design.

Right: Illustration for *The New York Times*.

Middle top: Announcement for an exhibition of 12 murals with the theme, "Eleven Books of the Century," commissioned by The New York Public Library in New York City. The murals were created by enlarging cut paper photographically into panels measuring 10' by 30' and illustrated 150 books of this century chosen by New York librarians.

Middle bottom: One of the murals from the exhibition. The books illustrated from left to right are: *My Fight for Birth Control, Dust Tracks on the Road, The Color Purple,* and *I Know Why the Caged Bird Sings.* Exhibition designer: Lou Storey

THE NEW YORK PUBLIC LIBRARY

Bottom left: Illustration for *Atlantic City* magazine.

Bottom right: Illustration for *The Wall Street Journal.*

Portfolio

Ron Blalock

5019 Swinton Drive
Fairfax, VA 22032
Phone: 703. 764.2071
Fax: 703. 764.0187

Ron Blalock uses scratchboard, ink, and pencil to produce his editorial illustrations, covers, spots, logos, and icons. His client list includes several large corporations, numerous design firms and associations.

Right: Cover for brochure for the Annenberg/CPB Multimedia Collection.
Design firm: Levine and Associates, Inc

Above: Editorial illustration that shows the liability and dangers of giving former employees bad reviews. Produced for the National Association of Temporary and Staffing Services.
Design firm: MacVicar Design & Communications, Inc.

Bottom left: Generic fall illustration for clip art publisher Dynamic Graphics.

Bottom right: Unpublished illustration.

Emanuel Schongut
Box 247
Mountain Dale, NY 12763
Phone: 914. 434.8964

Emanuel Schongut works in watercolor, pencil, and pen and ink media. His advertising and editorial illustrations have appeared in *New York, Esquire, Newsday, Redbook, Vogue, Bazaar* and *The New York Times*. He has created book jackets for Harper and Row, MacMillan, Morrow Books, Doubleday, and Green Willow Books for children and young adults.

Some of his most notable recent work has been posters for Mobil Masterpiece Theater, and Mobil Mystery Theater including posters for *Rebecca, Secret Agent, Portrait of a Marriage* and "Prime Suspect I and 11".

Pushpin Studios represented Schongut during his years in New York City.

Top left: Illustration for an article on roof gardens. *New York* magazine.

Top right: Illustration for an article on decorator pillows, "The Pillow Case," by Jane Geniesse. *New York* magazine.

Middle: Illustration for an article on "Sunday Composers." *New York* magazine.

Bottom left: Illustration for a book of short stories, *Baleful Beasts: Great Supernatural Stories of the Animal Kingdom*. Lathrop, Lee & Shepard Publishers.

Bottom right: Illustration for an article, "The Best Tailors in New York City." *New York* magazine.

Right: Advertisement for American Express.
Illustrator: Diana Bryan

Right: Book jacket for a book published by Simon and Schuster.
Illustrator: Diana Bryan
Art Director/Designer: Lucille Chomowicz
Copyright © 1996 Simon & Schuster. "Permission granted by arrangement with Simon & Schuster Books for Young Readers, Simon & Schuster Children's Publishing Division."

Below: Cover for the *Guild News,* the national voice for graphic artists.
Illustrator: Diana Bryan

1.

The number three on the first page of this chapter is from the Fontek font called Bendigo Plain.

2.

The drop cap that appears on the first page of this chapter is also from the font Bendigo Plain.

3.

This icon for hints was drawn in FreeHand.

4.

This column was created in Photoshop with clip art from T'Maker and the add noise filter.

Chapter 4
Photographs and the Truth

"Rivalry Between the Pink Poodles," shows four year old dance students before
the performance in Cortland, New York. This photograph was a feature
for the *Cortland Standard,* a daily newspaper in central New York.
Photographer: Pam Benham

Chapter opener: The box camera is clip art from Past Tints
Antique Illustrations. The photographer and bird were drawn by George Rhoads.

Photographs and the Truth

"We 'read' photographs... We bring to a picture a whole set
of personal and social associations. It is these 'meanings'
that are conjured up that make up the perception."

—Victor Burgia, *Photography, Fantasy, Function*, 1980.

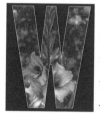e think of the painter or illustrator as a person who re-creates or interprets the world for the viewer. We think of the photographer as the person who, in the simple act of depressing a button, captures the world as it really exists. The camera has always been considered a reliable, faithful witness. A photograph places the viewer in a certain place and time. It has credibility.

In 1861, an English critic wrote, "Hitherto photography has been principally content with representing Truth." He went on to encourage photographers to produce pictures "whose aim is not merely to amuse, but to instruct, purify, and ennoble."

People believe a photograph and assume they are looking at the truth, or reality. Research has proven that photographs are the first, second, and third items that a reader looks at in the newspaper. Photographs in a publication can be an extremely powerful communication tool—an effective way to document and inform the reader of a particular event. Newspapers use photographs because they are reporting real events that happened with real people. A successful two-page photographic spread with good clear photographs and captions can tell an entire story without the need for any other words.

PHOTOGRAPHS VS. DRAWINGS OR OTHER ILLUSTRATIONS

A photograph will communicate a message in an obviously different way from a drawing. A photograph of victims of war will have a more powerful affect on us than a drawing because we know the people are real, not created out of the imagination or interpreted by the artist. If emotional impact is what you are after for your printed piece, a photograph will provide that. If your publication is a magazine and the articles relate to known figures such as the President or Madonna, your viewer will not be satisfied with a drawing. Photographs let us be voyeurs. We want to eavesdrop on celebrities, take a peak at their lives. The camera gives us access to that information. Photographs enable us to participate in the drama of daily life. If newspapers decided to use drawings instead of photographs, they would probably lose their readership.

A drawing gives us the artist's interpretation of the events. Photographs would provide the best record of a courtroom scene and all the players involved, but since a flash bulb going off in a courtroom can be disruptive during a trial, artists are sometimes hired to make quick sketches of the people involved. They provide a visual record of the events including the emotions on the faces of the defendants, the lawyers, and others.

This photograph gives the viewer an idea of the relationship between this well-dressed New York City woman and her dog.
Photographer: Harry Lapow
© Marcelle Lapow Toor

WHEN SHOULD YOU USE A PHOTOGRAPH?

Photographs should be used in publications where the reader needs to be given information about an actual event. They should be used in instances where a drawing will not provide for an intensity of emotion from the reader—the devastation from a forest fire, survivors of a war, the aftermath of an earthquake, a sports event, an automobile accident, a beautiful landscape. A significant factor in the decision to use a photograph over a drawing, chart or graph is the audience for the piece being designed. Stockholders as readers of annual reports want to see photographs of the people who are responsible for their invested money. They want to see photographs of the products or services offered by these corporations. Magazines use photographs of famous people on their covers to attract attention.

A good dramatic photograph will attract attention like no other illustration.

A photograph needs to:

- Appeal to the intended audience
- Attract attention
- Engage the interest of the viewer
- Be unambiguous
- Tell a story visually
- Be cropped well to eliminate unnecessary information
- Provide a focal point or entry to the printed page
- Be sharp and crisp for reproduction

You can change the meaning and the impact of a photograph by cropping it.

TRICKS TO USE WHEN WORKING WITH POOR QUALITY PHOTOGRAPHS

If the quality of the photograph you want to use is not clear and crisp, there are some tricks that can be done in an image-editing program like Photoshop.

You can:

1. Eliminate the entire background and silhouette an important part of the image.

2. Drop the photograph into a box or put it in a shaped box in order to hide the unnecessary parts of the photograph.

3. Replace the original background with another background, either one you create in an image-editing program or one from another photograph.

4. Retouch the photograph in Photoshop or another image-editing program and sharpen the image.

5. Convert a poor color photograph to black and white.

6. Scan the photograph and gray it out. This can either be done in an image-editing program or in your page layout program.

7. Gray out the photograph and have it bleed off the page. By doing this the photograph creates an atmosphere, and you get a sense of the photograph but you see it more as texture or a pattern in the background.

8. Have part of the photograph breaking out of a box.

9. Scan the photograph and use some of the filters in Photoshop (emboss, posterize, noise).

The photograph on the left is the original. The one on the right has been altered in Photoshop with the noise filter.
Photographer: Marcelle Lapow Toor

10. **Convert a color photograph to black and white.**

11. **Change the mode in an image-editing program from grayscale (halftone) to bitmap. This will eliminate the dots and the grays and change the photograph to lines, making it look more like a drawing.**

The quality of the photograph is important if you want your design to look professional. In order to reproduce well, a photograph should be sharp and have good contrast. A photograph printed on glossy paper stock will reproduce best. The size, placement, composition, and cropping of the photograph all contribute to its effectiveness and its impact.

Things to consider when using photographs:

1. **Size**

    A tiny photograph obviously will not have the impact of a larger one. A photograph contains information. The area with the information should be as large as you can possibly afford in terms of space and the other elements that exist on the page.

2. **Cropping**

    When using a photograph for a design layout, cropping is essential. You want a strong image that will get the attention of your viewer. In order to make a powerful statement, photographs need to be edited just like words. Cropping a photograph can turn a weak image into a stronger, more effective one. If there are outer portions in the photograph that do not relate to the story being illustrated, they should be eliminated.

    Photographers use L's (see illustration) cut out of mat or illustration board to use as a frame around the area of a photograph that has the greatest amount of appeal. The L's can be moved around the photograph until you identify an area within the frame that looks interesting. Marks, or masking tape, can be put around the extraneous parts to show the person who will be doing the pre-press work for the final printing

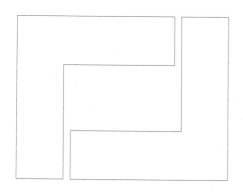

L's for cropping photographs.

which part of the photograph should be cropped.

If you are using a scanner to screen photographs, you will need to use an image-editing program to make adjustments for printing. Scan only the area of the photograph you need. If a photograph has already been scanned, cropping can be done in an image-editing program or your page layout program.

3. Direction of the action

The action of the photograph should lead the reader into the story or article, not off the page. You can direct the reader's eye to the information on the page by having the photograph facing in the direction you want the reader's eye to go.

The four ways to obtain photographs:

1. Take them yourself

If you are a competent photographer and you feel your publication should have photographs, take them yourself.

2. Hire a photographer

If you have a budget and time, commission the photographs you need from a professional photographer. Interview some photographers and look at portfolios to make sure you are hiring the right person for the job (see advice on hiring an illustrator, chapter 3, Drawings as Illustrations).

3. Go to a stock agency

If you don't need photographs of specific people in your organization, a stock agency may be the place for you. Stock agencies have archives of photographs in many different categories. If, for example, you need a photograph of a woman playing tennis, a stock agency should be able to help you. They charge a fee for one-time use of photographs.

4. Use clip art from disks, CD-ROMs, and books

Photographs of a variety of different subjects are available on disk or CD-ROM or in books. Most of these photographs, generic in subject matter, can be used with or without a fee depending on the source.

Sources of digital photo stock images:

Comstock
30 Irving Place
New York, NY 10003
Phone: 800. 225.2727

Corbis Media
15395 SE 30th Place, Suite 300
Bellevue, WA 98007
Phone: 800. 260.0444

Corel Corporation
1600 Carling Avenue
Ottawa, Ontario, Canada K1Z 8R7
Phone: 800. 772.6735

Dynamic Graphics
6000 North Forest Park Drive
Peoria, IL 61614
Phone: 800. 255.8800

Digital Stock Corporation
400 South Sierra Avenue, Suite 100
Salana Beach, CA 92075
Phone: 800. 545.4515

The Stock Market
360 Park Avenue south
New York, NY 10010
Phone: 800. 999.0800

If you are looking to hire a photographer, there are several books that will help you locate the person for your job:

American Photography Showcase

American Showcase, Inc.
724 Fifth Avenue, 10th floor
New York, NY 10019
Phone: 212. 245.0981

American Society of Magazine Photographers

419 Park Avenue South, Ste. 1407
New York, NY 10016
Phone: 212. 614.9644

Creative Sourcebook

Circulation Department
4085 Chain Bridge Road, Ste. 400
Fairfax, VA 22030-4106
Phone: 703. 385.5600

Photographer's Dispatch

AG Editions
142 Bank Street #GA
New York, NY 10014
Phone: 212. 929.0959

The Creative Black Book

Friendly Press, Inc.
401 Park Avenue South
New York, NY 10016
Phone: 212. 684.4255

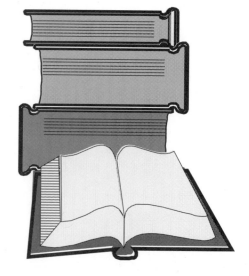

The books are clip art from T'Maker's Click Art Series. The color was removed and changed to different tints in FreeHand.

Photography began over a century and a half ago is now caught up in the digital revolution. This chapter deals with photographs as "the truth," but how will we begin to feel about photographs knowing that they can be manipulated on the computer? A photograph can be scanned into an image-editing program and altered so that one person's head is on another person's body— people can be placed in a photograph in a place they have never been (see chapter 6, Computer Graphics).

This graphic is from the Fontek font called DF Industrial One, typeset at 500 points.

Portfolio

Pam Benham
960 Buttercup Road
Hailey, ID 83333
Phone: 208. 788.3694
Fax: 208. 788.5919

Pam Benham is a freelance photographer based in Hailey, Idaho. She began her career as a photojournalist and now works for corporations and advertising agencies. Her client list includes US West Communications, Idaho Lottery, *Boise* magazine, the Wood River Medical Center, Orpheus West, Idaho Department of Agriculture, National Education Association, and Pacific Power.

Top right: Americana Barn Series.

Bottom left: Photograph for an ad campaign for Farmers National Bank.

Bottom right: Photograph for a photo essay on male strippers for the *Cortland Standard*.

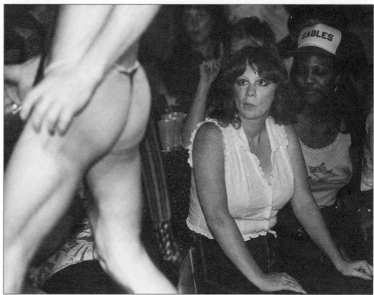

Top: Poster, "Seven Pounds."
Client: The Children's Defense Fund.
Creative Director: Bill Westbrook
Art Director: Tom Lichtenheld
Photographer: Buck Holzemer
Copywriter: Sally Hogshead
Agency: Fallon McElligott

Cover for 1993 Annual Report
Client: UNIFEM
Designers: Lisa LaRochelle, Jurek Wajdowicz
Art director: Jurek Wajdowicz
Photographer: Sebastião Salgado
Design firm: Emerson, Wajdowicz Studios

How did she do that?

A list of the graphic devices used in this chapter and how each was created

1.

The number four is from the typeface, called Helvetica Compressed. It was typed in FreeHand and converted to paths. The photograph to the right was scanned into Photoshop and imported into FreeHand. The photograph was cut out and pasted into the four.

2.

The W was treated the same way as the number four.

3.

This camera is a clip art image from T/Maker's Click Art Series.

4.

The column on the left was created by putting the clip art camera into Photoshop and using the embossing filter.

Chapter 5
Using
Information Graphics

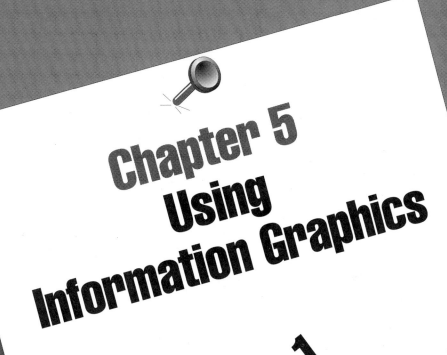

Illustration created for the the American Society of Quality Control, Milwaukee, WI.
Illustrator: Leslie Cober Gentry, Trumbull, CT

Chapter opener: The map is clip art from Past Tints Antique Illustrations.
The chart is from T'Maker's Click Art Series.

Using Information Graphics

igel Holmes, the designer who created the information graphics—the charts, graphs, and diagrams we saw in *Time* magazine—says that statistical information should be turned into "a visual idea rather than a tedious parade of numbers. Without being frivolous, I want to entertain the reader as well as inform."

Information graphics—charts, graphs, tables, maps, and diagrams—are a way to add visual or graphic interest to a page while providing statistical data. Information graphics have become a significant presence in our information-ridden society. Charts, graphs, diagrams, maps, tables, and other visual displays of data provide a means to present facts that cannot be shown with drawings, photographs, or other forms of illustrations.

Information graphics have a long history. In the 11th century, charts were used to show the orbits of planets. Maps were used early in our history to indicate location and direction. Edward Tufte, author of several books on the presentation of statistical information, says of information graphics, "Graphical excellence is that which gives the viewer the greatest number of ideas in the shortest time with the least ink in the smallest space...Data graphics should draw the viewer's attention to the sense and substance of the data, not to something else."

On September 15, 1982, *USA Today* made its first appearance on news stands—an event that sent off reverberations throughout the entire newpaper industry. *USA Today* was the first newspaper to use charts and graphs to help readers grasp complex information quickly. The newspaper has made an impact on the newspaper and magazine world. We talk about the "*USA Today* look" when we refer to the use of illustrative charts and graphs as a means of presenting information.

Charts, graphs, maps, diagrams, and tables should be used to illustrate data that may otherwise be uninteresting. The illustrator or designer's role in the creation of information graphics is to present the information in a way that is aesthetically pleasing, illuminating, and easy to read and understand at first glance.

WHICH FORMAT SHOULD YOU USE?
What are the options?
1. Bar and column charts

Bar and column charts provide a good format to show comparisons in a way that is easily identifiable. The data can be displayed in horizontal or vertical bars or columns.

2. Pie charts

Pie charts, charts created in the form of a circle or oval and cut into wedges like a pie, are a good way to show data or information as parts of the whole.

3. Diagrams

Diagrams are used as a method of showing how a system works. It is a way of translating complicated events or concepts into a simplified drawing.

4. Graphs

Like charts, graphs are used to present information and show comparisons. Lines are used in place of bars.

This chart is clip art from Image Club Graphics Woodcut series. It has been altered slightly.

5. Illustrative graphs and charts

Illustrative graphs use pictographs instead of lines and bars. They are used to show comparisons to an audience that is visually oriented. The illustrative graph displays information through the use of pictorial images related to the data.

6. Maps

Maps, one of the oldest means of graphic communication, are used to indicate locations. Maps provide information that is geographical, topographical, and geological in nature. They are good illustrations to use when you want to show directions to a specific place or to indicate a hard to find location. Maps can provide an interesting backgound pattern for a printed piece that needs to look more graphic.

7. Tables

Tables display data containing information of importance to the viewer in the form of lists. Tables are simpler and easier to design than charts or graphs but need to be designed for easy readability. They are used to display daily items in newspapers for the weather, the stock market report, baseball and football scores, and other items of interest to their readers. The information in a table should be organized well, in clearly defined columns, and use a readable typeface. Labels or headlines should be used to identify the information being displayed.

8. Bulleted lists

Bulleted lists show related items that do not have a specific order.

9. Numbered lists

Numbered lists are used to indicate related items that have a definite order.

Charts and graphs come in all sizes and shapes. Some use pictographs, some lines, some bars. There are several things you

The checks in the bulleted list are from Adobe's Zapf Dingbats.

need to consider before you make a decision about the format and style of your chart or graph.

CHECKLIST FOR USING INFORMATION GRAPHICS

The following questions in the bulleted list should help you decide on the format and design of the statistical graphic for your printed piece.

✔ Who is the audience?

✔ What is the style of your printed piece (informal, formal)?

✔ What do you want to convey? Do you need to show a comparison, parts of a whole, a list in sequential order, diagrams, location?

✔ What format, chart, graph, map, or table will make your data clear and easy to read?

✔ Who will create this graphic? If the information you need to present is complex and beyond your abilities, you may want to hire an illustrator to create your graphic.

Several software programs will convert your statistical information into graphs and charts. The numerical information is entered, and the program sorts it out and turns it into a bar chart or other chart or graph of your choice. The graphs and charts produced by these programs have a "canned" look and should be reworked in a drawing program for a more professional look.

Adobe Illustrator, Chartmaker, and Corel Draw are some software programs for creating charts and graphs.

Maps on disk

Maps can be used to identify specific places and can also be used to provide background texture.

Right: This globe on a tripod is from an old wood engraving. It is clip art from Harter Image Archives.

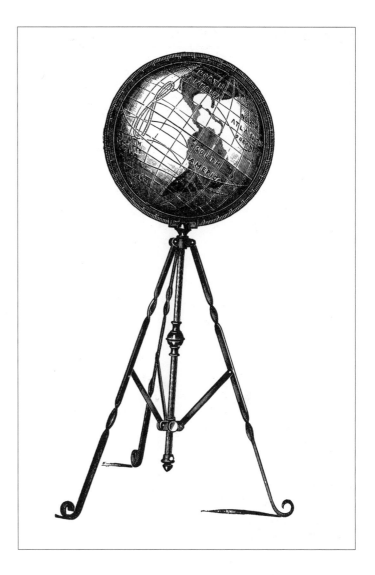

Below: These maps are clip art images from Cartesia. They are available on CD-ROM.

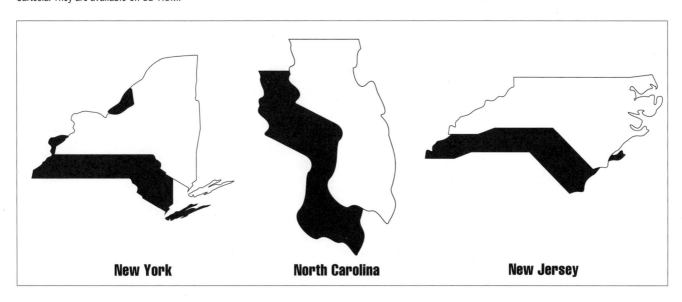

New York   **North Carolina**   **New Jersey**

Bar chart

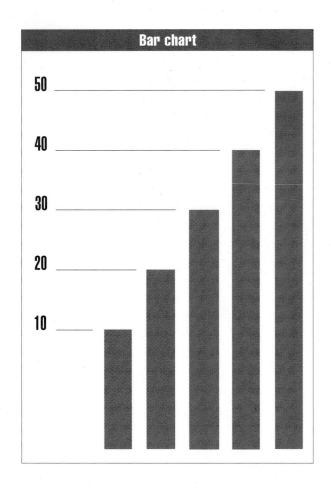

Pictorial chart

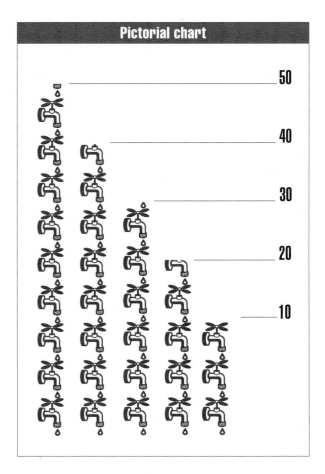

The charts above were created in FreeHand. They both contain the same information, but the one on the right uses a graphic to illustrate the information.

The curve chart on the right uses textures as a way of illustrating different information.

The pie chart below breaks data into pieces of a whole.

Pie Chart

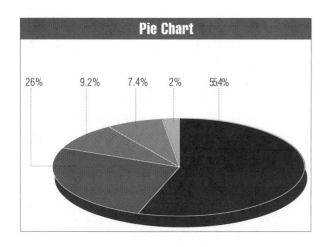

26%   9.2%   7.4%   2%   55.4%

Curve chart

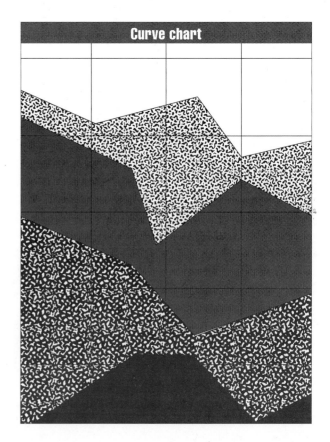

This diagram is from a monograph, *Breaking the Glass Ceiling,* by Renée Broderick, for Cornell University's School of Industrial and Labor Relations. It is a model of management career systems and demonstrates the information in a diagram with simple stylized figures—pictograms rather than a chart or graph.
Illustrator: Marcelle Lapow Toor

Illustrated chart for an article, "What's Your Worth?" showing results of the 1993 *How* magazine graphic arts salary survey, February 1994.
Illustrator: Leslie Cober Gentry

MANAGEMENT HIERARCHY

EXECUTIVE SEARCH FIRMS
REFERRAL NETWORKS
(External source)
EXECUTIVE SUCCESSION PLANS
(Internal source)

TOP MANAGEMENT

SEARCH FIRMS
REFERRAL NETWORKS
(External source)
HIGH POTENTIAL LISTS
(Internal source)

MIDDLE MANAGEMENT

COLLEGE RECRUITING
REFERRAL NETWORKS
(External source)

ENTRY MANAGEMENT

AVERAGE SALARY

Males $40,896

Females $33,406

Metro Area $38,078

Non-Metro $31,566

Pictorial chart

This pictorial chart shows the armed forces in World War II. The illustration was created for "Our Times, the Illustrated History of the 20th Century" for Turner/CNN.
Illustrator: Nigel Holmes

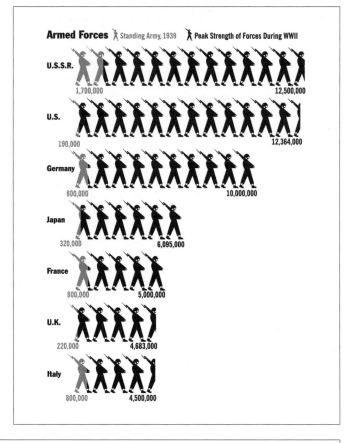

Armed Forces ⚔ Standing Army, 1939 ⚔ Peak Strength of Forces During WWII

U.S.S.R. 1,700,000 12,500,000

U.S. 190,000 12,364,000

Germany 800,000 10,000,000

Japan 320,000 6,095,000

France 800,000 5,000,000

U.K. 220,000 4,683,000

Italy 800,000 4,500,000

Diagram

Diagram for *The New York Times* to illustrate the 1995 Gallileo mission to Jupiter.
Illustrator: Nigel Holmes

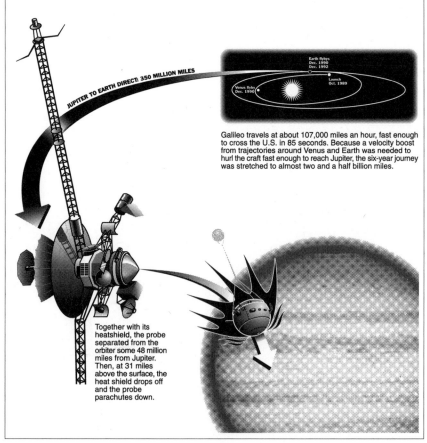

JUPITER TO EARTH DIRECT: 350 MILLION MILES

Earth flybys
Dec. 1990
Dec. 1992

Venus flyby
Dec. 1990

Launch
Oct. 1989

Galileo travels at about 107,000 miles an hour, fast enough to cross the U.S. in 85 seconds. Because a velocity boost from trajectories around Venus and Earth was needed to hurl the craft fast enough to reach Jupiter, the six-year journey was stretched to almost two and a half billion miles.

Together with its heatshield, the probe separated from the orbiter some 48 million miles from Jupiter. Then, at 31 miles above the surface, the heat shield drops off and the probe parachutes down.

Maps

Right: Map showing sizes of states in proportion to the amount of media coverage (*The New York Times* and *Network News*) for the 1984 election campaign. This map was used in the book, *Pictorial Maps* by Nigel Holmes.
Illustrator: Nigel Holmes

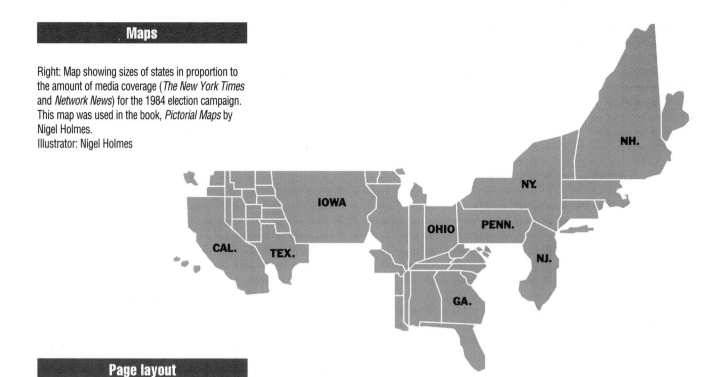

Page layout

Bottom: Two page spread from *Wordperfect* magazine.
Art director: Don Lambson
Designer: Don Lambson
Illustrator: Seymour Chwast
Agency: *Wordperfect* magazine

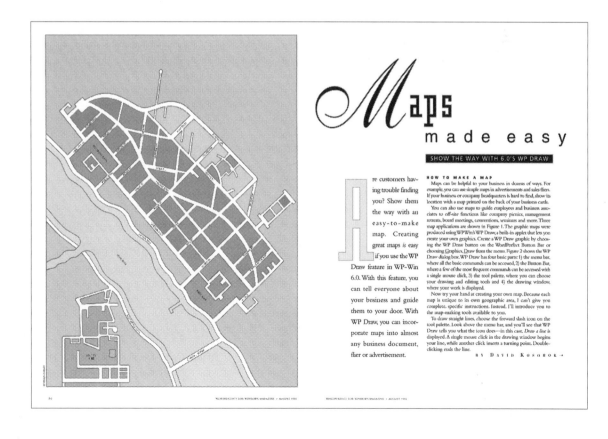

1.

The number in the chapter opener was created in FreeHand. The box in the background is from a clip art chart. A line was drawn and duplicated.

2.

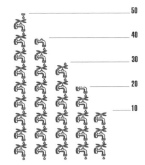

The same box graphic was used for the drop cap on the first page of this chapter. The lines were drawn in FreeHand.

3.

This chart was created in FreeHand using the pictorial font DF Naturals, from Fontek.

4.

The column on the left was created by placing the chart graphic into Photoshop and using the dust and scratch, and pointillize filters.

Chapter 6
Computer Graphics

Poster for the New York City Opera National Company's performance of "The Marriage of Figaro."
Designer: David Sigman

Chapter opener: Clip art image from T'Maker's Click Art Series.

Computer Graphics

"The best designers are constantly finding ways of making non-obvious adjustments that add depth and character to bland art."
—Steve Hannaford, *Print.* March/April 1995.

he painting and drawing programs that we first experienced in the mid-1980s were awkward and often clumsy to use but the "wow" factor was there and those of us who were beginning to use computers at that time were awed by the tasks the computer could accomplish. The technology has changed—the old programs have been upgraded and replaced with ones that are more sophisticated, more complex, and powerful—ones that require skill and a great deal of computer memory. The computer has become a new useful tool for illustrators and designers. Intricate and complicated tasks, difficult and impossible to do by hand, can be carried out on the computer.

Many illustrators who began their careers before 1985 are using the computer to supplement their pens, paints, pastels, and other traditional tools. Some have laid the old tools to rest and are working directly on the computer. Others tend to use both the old and new tools in conjunction with each other—working out ideas and concepts for illustrations on paper with pen or pencil, going to the scanner, and from there to a drawing or painting program to refine the finished product by adding type and other elements. Since many designers are designing directly on the

This brush stroke simulation is from T/Maker.

computer, graphics generated on the computer make the design and printing process faster, easier, and considerably less expensive. They save steps in the final printing process. Final page designs are camera-ready and an entire publication can be given to a printer on disk.

PAINTING VS. DRAWING PROGRAMS

There are two different types of software programs that can be used for rendering illustrations—painting programs and drawing programs. They work quite differently from each other. Often these programs are used in conjunction with image-editing and scanning software. Before purchasing a program for creating your illustrations you need to identify your task and select a program(s) that will help you accomplish your illustration goal(s).

■ **Painting programs (raster or bit-mapped)**

Painting programs simulate traditional media. Colors can be mixed on the monitor in much the same way as on a palette, except you don't get your hands wet or dirty. You do not have to wait hours or days for the paint to dry. You can get effects that look like watercolor, crayon, oil, and pastel. Brush strokes can be customized to your needs. Images can be easily duplicated, superimposed, and combined with other images to create a collage.

When you use a painting program, the pixels—the dots that make up the image—will be evident (you will see the jagged edges). The resolution you see on your monitor is what will print out, the WYSIWYG (what you see is what you get) factor, unless your piece is printed at a high resolution. Type set in a painting program will not appear sharp and crisp.

Advantages of using a painting program
☛ **Painting programs are relatively easy to use**

Painting programs are fairly intuitive. You do not have to be a technical genius to figure out the software. You do not have to spend hours reading the manual to figure out how to use the many different features. Ideas are easy to work out.

The tool boxes that come with painting programs have icons that are self-explanatory

Painting programs offer tools that resemble traditional tools, and the icons in the tool box help you identify them easily.

Special effects are easy to achieve

Painting programs give you the ability to achieve special effects that you cannot get with drawing programs: pastel, brushstroke, wet paint, watercolor, and spray paint.

Drawing freehand is easy

It is easy to draw regular and irregular lines, as well as different kinds of geometric shapes.

Erasing is easy

The eraser works like a real eraser and will erase parts of your painting. Erasing is not easy in a drawing program.

Colors can be easily blended

With the airbrush tool you can spray one color or blend colors. You have access to over 16 million colors.

Disadvantages of using a painting program

Sophisticated painting programs require a great deal of computer memory

If you do not have a powerful computer with lots of RAM and ROM, rendering a complex illustration will be slow going and your graphic will consume a lot of memory.

The final output will show jagged edges

If your illustration is not being printed on a high resolution printer, the jagged edges will be evident. This is not a problem if that is the effect you wish to achieve.

Fonts will not reproduce well

You can get some interesting effects with fonts in a

This computer is from the font called DF Industrials Two from Fontek.

painting program but if your publication is not printed on a printer with high resolution, the lines of your letters will look jagged.

SuperPaint, PixelPaint, Fractal Design Painter, and DeskPaint are some examples of the popular painting programs.

■ **Drawing programs (object-oriented or vector)**

Drawing programs are vector-based, as opposed to painting programs that are pixel based. This means that, when you use a drawing program, the computer remembers the x, y, and z coordinates for each line you create. Object oriented graphics created in a drawing program are defined by paths. Each line you draw follows a path. When the path is closed off you have a shape that can be filled with a color, texture, or pattern.

Drawing programs use the PostScript language code developed by Adobe Systems that enables the computer to communicate with a laser printer or other output device—imagesetter, or film processor. What you see on the computer monitor is not what you get when you work with a PostScript image. The printed results you get far exceed the resolution on your screen. The lines, type, and fills you use in your drawings will print out smooth and sharp. If you use graduated fills, the final output will show the continuous tones.

Advantages of using a drawing program

➤ Graphics maintain their integrity and clarity

Graphics imported into a page layout program can be resized, enlarged, or reduced, and will still retain their sharp, smooth lines.

➤ You get straight, not jagged lines

Diagonal, curved, or straight lines of varying thickness can be drawn, changed, and customized.

➤ Different objects and shapes can be created and filled

A shape or object is created by going from one end of a

path and coming full circle to the beginning of the path. This is similar to the connect-the-dots books young children enjoy. When the objects are completely closed they can be filled with any number of available textures or customized fills and colors.

You can create layers

Drawing programs work with layers. Each time you create a line or object a layer is established. Objects or lines can be added. Complex drawings can be rendered in this way.

You can alter existing clip art

Most of the clip art available on disk has been created in a drawing program: FreeHand, Illustrator, or CorelDraw. The clip art image you want can be brought into one of these programs and changes made so that it will look like it had been rendered solely for your printed piece. Since so many of us use clip art, and so many of the ready-made images look canned, a drawing program is invaluable for customizing images for your needs.

High resolution output from any printer

Graphics created in drawing programs can be resized in your page layout program without losing resolution. The resolution from any PostScript printer will be good.

Disadvantages

Long learning process

Drawing programs are not intuitive. In order to use the full capability of your program you must read the manual—not an easy task for most of us who want instant gratification. Manuals are often written by people with technical know-how but cannot communicate information well. Publishers like Ventana Press, Peachpit Press, and others are producing manuals for many of the popular software programs. The manuals are easy to understand, are inexpensive, and will save you a great deal of time.

THINGS TO CONSIDER WHEN CHOOSING AN ILLUSTRATION PROGRAM

1. What is the task you wish to accomplish?

If you want to render line drawings for a flyer or brochure, you will need a drawing program. If you want your drawings to have a painterly look, a painting program may suit you better.

2. What kind of computer will you use?

Before selecting a drawing or painting program, you need to know how much memory—RAM and ROM—is in your computer. The program you are considering may not work on your computer if it is low on memory. Graphics take up large amounts of memory. If your computer does not have sufficient memory to handle a powerful program, your system could crash.

3. Which drawing/painting program is best for you?

Many illustration programs can be used across computer platforms. Each program has its own specific features. Find out what the features are and select the program that offers the most capabilities for the tasks you need to regularly perform. Visit your local computer dealer(s) and ask for demonstrations of the programs you are considering. Ask to see hard copy of graphics done in those programs.

File formats for saving and printing computer generated graphics

Graphics that are not formatted properly cannot be brought into other programs. If you have created a graphic for use in your page layout or drawing program, you need to know how to save it so that the program you are using will acknowledge and recognize it. The graphics you create must also be compatible with the final printing process you will be using. There are several different formatting options you can use based on your computer, the programs you are using, and your needs.

EPS (Encapsulated PostScript)

If you want to import graphics—drawings, charts, graphs,

type for drop caps, or type as illustration—into your page layout program (PageMaker, Quark XPress, Ventura Publisher), they should be saved as EPS files. Saving them in this format will enable you to resize and rotate them to fit into your design. They will maintain their integrity and reproduce well in black-and-white or color.

PICT format

PICT files support bit-map images and will take up much more room in your page layout program than other file formats. Saving graphics in a PICT format is an option in many drawing and painting programs. Save graphics in this format while your work on an illustration is in progress. After you have completed your drawing export it or save it as an EPS file.

TIFF (Tag Image File Format)

TIFF format is used when saving grayscale images, photographs, drawings, or other images that have been scanned. TIFF graphics can be brought into an image editing program, drawing, or paint program. TIFF images can be altered and brought into a page layout program, where, depending on your program, special effects can be added. TIFF formatted images also print well in high resolution.

RIFF (Raster Image File Format)

The RIFF format is the PC equivalent to TIFF.

■ Image-editing programs

Adobe Photoshop, Micrografix Picture Publisher, Aldus Photostyler, and Fractal Design Color Studio are image-editing programs. They are digital darkrooms. They perform many functions of the old traditional darkroom and are chemical-free. A scanner and an image-editing program are a powerful duo for the illustrator and designer. Photographs that are underexposed or overexposed can be altered to gain more

TIP 1:

For special, interesting effects, enlarge an image or text on a copy machine. This will break up the details and create more of a pattern thus changing the appearance, and even the meaning of the original drawing or photograph. It is possible to take the enlarged, less defined image, scan it and play with it in an image-editing program.

TIP 2:

Create collages by blending different materials, textures, and images on the computer or scanner to achieve special graphics. In this way you can create images that are unique, appealing, and intriguing.

contrast. Parts of photographs can be removed to make the image stronger or to eliminate distracting portions in the original image.

Image-editing programs provide the illustrator or designer with more than a digital darkroom. Special effects can be applied to any image using various tools and filters such as extrude, pinch, noise, emboss, and others.

Creating special effects

The computer is an excellent tool when you want to create those special effects that will make your newsletter or brochure more visually exciting and compelling. Dramatic effects can be achieved with a scanner, photocopy machine, and an image-editing program.

Photographs and drawings, wrapping paper, and textured materials with interesting patterns can be scanned into an image-editing program where filters, such as noise, diffuse, pinch, mosaic, pointillize, blur, shear, find edges, extrude, emboss, distort displace, dispeckle, and others, will alter the image in different ways. You can get other special effects with the various tools in the toolbox as well: airbrush, brush, rubber stamp, smudge, and blur and sharpen. You can get three dimensional effects by creating shadows for your text and pictures.

Using a scanner

A scanner is an essential piece of equipment if you expect to be creating your own illustrations or using photographs for your publications. If you are better at drawing graphics by hand but want to put them into your computer to use in your printed piece, you can draw them, scan them into an image-editing program, and bring them into a drawing or painting program.

Part of a newspaper was scanned in Photoshop. The word newspaper was typed in FreeHand, converted to paths and the scan was pasted into the word.

NEWSPAPER

The word shadow, was typeset in FreeHand, filled with 60 percent gray and put into Photoshop where the gaussian blur filter was used to create a soft blur. The words were typed again in Photoshop and placed on top of the blurred ones.

Soft shadow

Soft Shadow

The words, graduated fill, were typeset in Photoshop. Each letter was filled with the gradual fill tool.

Graduated fill

Graduated fill

The unsharp mask filter was added to the graduated fill above and the embossing filter was applied.

Graduated fill—embossed

Graduated Fill

The word, separated, was typeset in Photoshop. The middle section was selected with the rectangle tool and moved slightly to the right. The feather feature was used to soften the lines. The same thing was done with the bottom half of the word.

Cutting, pasting, and feathering

SEPARATED

Radial fill

The words, radial fill, were typed in FreeHand and converted to paths and radial fill was applied.

Zoom text

The words were typeset in FreeHand and the zoom text from the type dialog box was selected.

Patterned fill

The M on the left is from the font called Bendigo. It was typeset in FreeHand, converted to paths where the patterned fill (heavy mezzo) was added.

Joined elements

Left: The M and T are from the font called Helvetica Compressed. They were typeset separately, converted to paths, and the "join elements" feature was selected, creating the intersecting effect.

Right: The M and T are from the font called Dolmen. This design was created the same way as the one on its left.

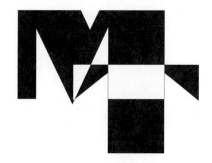

The text was typeset in FreeHand. A circle was drawn and ungrouped. It was then cut in half and the lower half was deleted. Both the text and the arc were selected and the "bind to path" feature was applied.

The text in a circle was treated the same way as the one above but the circle was left in tact and the text placed around it.

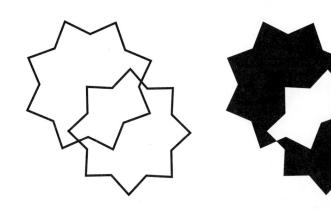

Left: One object was drawn using the star tool in FreeHand. This object was duplicated and the second one was placed on top of the other. Right: The two objects were duplicated and filled with black. The "join objects" feature was selected and the overlapped portion was punched out.

Joined objects

The object on the left was drawn and the "flow inside a path" option was applied. The text was typed right into the object. The object on the left was filled with 50% gray and flipped to create the negative space in the middle.

Text flowed inside a path

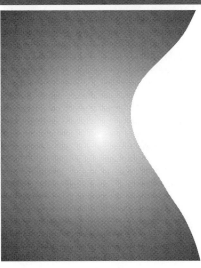

This is an example of text that has been placed inside a path. This is an example of text that has been placed inside a path. This is an example of text that has been placed inside a path. This is an example of text that has been placed inside a path. This is an example of text that has been placed inside a path. This is an example of text that has been placed inside a path.This is an example of text that has been placed inside a path. This is an example of text that has been placed inside a path. This is an example of text that has been placed inside a path. This is an example of text that has been placed inside a path. This is an example of text that has been placed inside a path. This is an example of text that has been placed inside a path. This is an This is an example of text that has been placed inside a path. This is an example of text that has been placed inside a path. This is an example of text that has been placed inside a path. This is an example of text

Special effects with photographs

The original photograph of buildings in downtown Montreal with reflections was scanned into Photoshop. Different filters were applied in the two altered photographs below and on the opposite page.

Top right: Original photograph
Photographer: Marcelle Lapow Toor, 1995.

Bottom left: The "difference clouds" filter in Photoshop was added to the background of the original photograph to create a mysterious cloudy effect.

Bottom right: The original photograph with text added. The word, Montreal was typeset in Photoshop and filled with gray. The "add noise" filter was applied.

Top right: The "extrude" filter applied to the original photograph.

Bottom left: The "invert" command.

Bottom right: The "emboss" filter.

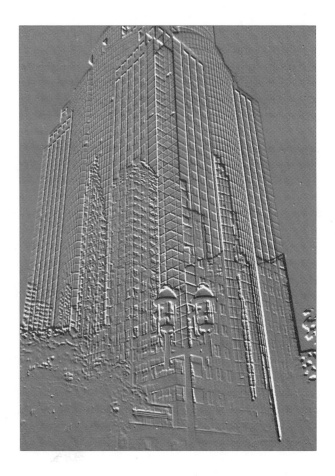

An illusion of depth can be created in a drawing program, or you can use a 3-D program to give that sense of perspective and to add another dimension to what would otherwise be a two-dimensional drawing.

TriSpectives, a new software program for the PC, enables the illustrator to create detailed 3-D drawings, or models that can be used for presentations, printed materials, animation, and multimedia projects.

The illustrations on this page were created in TriSpectives as clip art by Cornell University students.

Top: Jack-in-the-box.
Artist: Tai Park
Content Coordinator: Nancy Heinz

Middle: Lawn chair.
Artist: Simeon Netchev
Content Coordinator: Nancy Heinz

Bottom: Native American baskets.
Artist: Nancy Heinz

Creating background textures

Background textures or patterns provide a good, inexpensive way to be illustrative, to dress up a document, and to make a page more interesting visually. Any patterned material can be scanned into an image-editing program to get an interesting texture.

Top right: Original wrapping scanned.

Bottom left: The tile filter was applied to the original scanned wrapping paper.

Bottom right: The tiled wrapping paper on the left screened using Image Control in PageMaker.

Original wrapping paper

Tile filter—black

Tile filter with screen—70% black

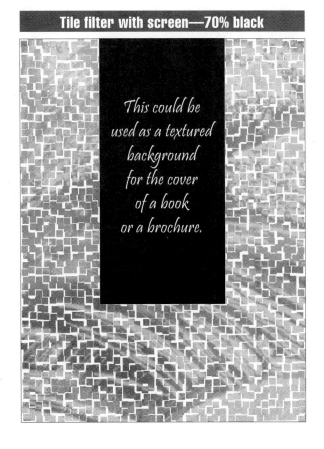

This could be used as a textured background for the cover of a book or a brochure.

Portfolio

Office of Publications Services
Cornell University
East Hill Plaza
Ithaca, NY 14850
Phone: 607. 255.4945
Fax: 607. 255.5684

Cornell's Office of Publications Services is responsible for editing, and designing many of the printed materials for the endowed colleges and administrative offices of the university.

Hazardous waste icons

These symbols have been taken from various sources and adapted to have a consistent look. They are used on Cornell Environmental Health and Safety posters outside laboratories throughout the University to indicate what hazards are found in the labs. The icons were created in FreeHand 5.0. Designer/Illustrator: Richard Howland-Bolton
Art Director: Sally Dutko

CHEMICAL STORAGE

FLAMMABLE SOLIDS

ELECTRICAL HAZARD

WATER REACTIVES

CORROSIVES

BIOHAZARD

Portfolio

Kathleen Chmelewski

2006 Boudreau Drive
Urbana, IL 61801
Phone: 217. 328.4303

Kathleen Chmelewski is an assistant professor in the Graphic Design and Photography Department at the University of Illinois at Urbana in Champaign.

Top right: "Early Years," one of three images from a commemorative installation at the Graduate School of Library and Information Science at the University of Illinois. The images celebrate the 100th year anniversary of the school, and chronicle the history of the field of Library Science and affiliated technologies with images.

Bottom right: "Recent Years"

Bottom left: "Lightning," a computer collage.

Barbara Nessim

63 Greene Street
New York, NY 10012
Phone: 212. 219.1111
Fax: 212. 219.0989

"The intuitive part of the Mac allows me to think about my work in a more expansive way. I love to draw on the computer. I think the computer is such a fascinating tool to incorporate into the thinking processes and the art that I am doing now."

Barbara Nessim's illustrations combine the ancient and the modern. She uses traditional artist's materials, pen and ink, gouache, pastels, and computers. In 1982, Nessim began using a computer. She feels the computer enables her to make quick and easy changes. She doesn't have to start from scratch each time she wants to redraw an image. And she can keep the original image intact.

Nessim creates drawings by hand in sketchbooks. She uses these drawings as inspiration for her commissioned illustrations and recreates them on the computer for the final product. Nessim sees the computer as another tool, part of her paint box, a way of electronically reproducing the pen and ink drawings in her sketchbooks.

The images on this page are from Nessim's 3D Books series, "Outside/Inside."

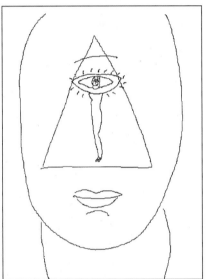

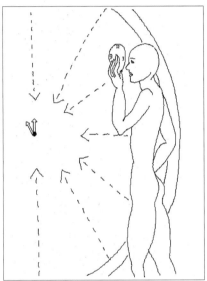

Top and bottom: Illustrations for an exhibition, "Random Access Memories, an Interactive Artwork Miniature Sketchbook." The images are supposed to be looked at through a viewer to get a 3D effect. © Barbara Nessim

Middle left: Center Peace. © Barbara Nessim

Middle right: Egg Timer. © Barbara Nessim

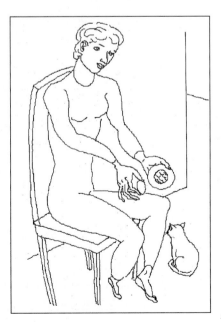

Hillustration

701 Estates Court
Bel Air, MD 21015
Phone: 410. 893.7620
Fax: 410. 893.7615

"I used to do all my scratchboard illustrations traditionally, but about two and a half years ago, I began producing them electronically. Working this way has allowed me greater flexibility. I can deliver files over the modem, and revisions are much easier. I also have the ability to explore more options with the art without damaging it in any way."

Mike Hill uses his own home page to "proof" artwork with clients that have access to the Web.

In order to preserve the "hand done" aspect of his work, he does a pencil sketch that he uses as a template, opens the sketch in Painter 4.0, and with the tracing paper feature, works up the artwork with a Wacom tablet and the scratchboard tool. He uses Photoshop and FreeHand.

Top right: Illustration for the Baltimore Gas and Electric newsletter for an article about making a home more energy efficient.

Bottom left: Illustration for *Entrepreneur* magazine for an article about business contracts.

Bottom right: Illustration for a Christmas card sent to clients.

Daniel Pelavin
80 Varick Street #3B
New York, NY 10013-1925
Phone: 212. 941.7418
Fax: 212. 431.7138

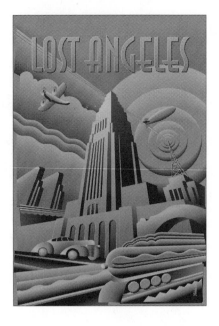

"I start every job by doing very loose thumbnail sketches with a fountain pen in an Aquabee No. 808 Super Deluxe sketchbook. I then scan them and use them as a template in Illustrator."

Daniel Pelavin, a New York City illustrator, has earned national recognition for his illustrations and designs from the American Institute of Graphic Arts, Graphis Poster, Society of Illustrators, *Print* magazine's Regional Design Annual, and others. He created the popular typeface, called ITC Anna, and a new font called Fatline bold.

Daniel Pelavin works on a Macintosh IIci daystar turbo 040, and uses Logitech Scanman and Adobe Illustrator 5.5.

Top left: Illustration designed as for a book cover for Oxford University Press.

Top right: Self-promotion.

Right: Editorial illustration for *Enterprise* magazine about new manufacturing technology.

Streetworks Studio

13908 Marblestone Drive
Clifton, VA 22024
Phone: 703. 631.1650
Fax: 703. 631.7420

Streetworks Studio is an illustration and design studio whose illustration styles range from cut paper silhouettes, watercolors, and linoleum block prints, to computer art. Their designs are created on their Macintosh computers. Their client list includes: *The Washington Post, U.S. News & World Report,* Mobil Oil, The National Institutes of Health, the Federal Trade Commission, and several other local agencies and design studios. Their work has appeared in many juried annuals.

Top left: Streetworks logo

Top right: Logo for the National Hispanic Leadership Initiative. Streetworks won a competition to design a graphic identity package for the National Hispanic Leadership Initiative on Cancer. The client loved the graphic and it was adopted as their logo.

Above: Logo used in a self-promotional brochure showing various Streetworks Studio logo designs.

Bottom right: Illustration for Minority Breast Cancer Awareness Day. This illustration was used on buttons, name tags, posters, and banners to promote Minority Breast Cancer Awareness Day.

Design & Illustration

National Hispanic Leadership Initiative on Cancer

a program of the National Cancer Institute

MINORITY BREAST CANCER AWARENESS DAY

Top: Hoover *Guide to the Top Chicago Companies.*
Designer/illustrator: Daniel Pelavin

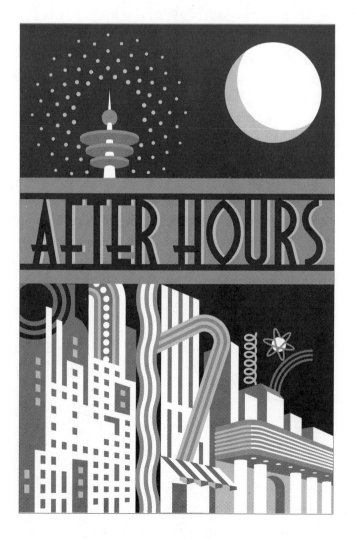

Left: *After Hours,* one of ten illustrations representing different types of
websites for *PC Magagine's* survey of the top 100 websites.
Designer/illustrator: Daniel Pelavin

Top: Cover for *Public Service Center Manual* for the
Public Service Center, Cornell. The art was created in
FreeHand 5.0 using several items, some from clip art
sources that were altered by converting to paths, and
stretching. Various parts of the illustration were used
throughout the manual to enloven the text.
Designer: Clive Howard
Art Director: Sally Dutko

The inside pages of the *Public Service Center Manual*
carry forth the style created on the cover and use
grayed out type and graphics.

How did she do that?

A list of the graphic devices used in this chapter and how each was created

1.

The number six and the drop cap on the first page of this chapter are from the Fontek font called Bitmax. A second six was placed behind the white one to give a shadow effect. The font was chosen for its "digital" look.

2.

This graphic is from the font called Fontek DF Industrials One.

3.

The tack/pushpin on the right has been used throughout this book for the chapter openers and tips. The original clip art (left), from T/Maker, has been altered in FreeHand by placing a radial filled oval on top of the tack to create a concave effect.

4. Left: Pieces of wrapping paper were cut and pasted into Photoshop and the wave filter was applied. It was placed onto this page in PageMaker and altered again using the image control feature in the element menu.

Chapter 7
Picture Sources

Illustration: "Four Scenes from the Life of a Dog in the Dog-Days,"
from *Harper's New Monthly Magazine*, Volume V,
June to November 1852. Illustrator unknown.

Chapter opener: The man on the bicycle is clip art from Past Tints Antique Illustrations.
The books are clip art from T/Maker. The map is clip art from Cartesia.
The copyright sign was created in FreeHand, converted to paths, and filled with a graduated fill.
The wagon was hand-drawn and scanned into Photoshop.

Picture Sources

"Historical prints cover an inexhaustible arrray
of subjects, ranging from fashions to hunting,
scenes of trade and industry, cities,
daily life and sentimental topics."
—Ann Novotny, Editor, Rosemary Eakins, *Picture Sources 3.* 1975.

ou have designed a brochure with an "old world" look. You need several illustrations that will reinforce that look—possibly some old woodcuts or drawings. Hiring an illustrator to create the effect you want is not in your budget. The art you have been searching for does not seem to be available in clip art on disk, CD-ROM, or in books. Where do you find those special images? There are several options.

This chapter contains a list of some available resources, both public and private.

1. Professional picture researchers

Professional picture researchers are people who maintain lists of sources and will help you locate those special images for a fee.

2. Public collections: libraries and museums

If you are on a tight budget you can be your own picture researcher. Many public libraries and museums have collections of pictures. You can do research in the library and request permission, in writing, to use the images you want. Some of these facilities have a photographic service and can give you prints of the pictures you want. You must obtain permission in order to use illustrations legally. You may have to pay to get reproduction rights. Some public institutions do not charge a fee but expect you to include a credit line acknowledging the organization.

3. Commercial picture libraries

Commercial picture libraries contain archives of different kinds of pictorial materials. Often these libraries have catalogs of their materials and will provide a researcher to help you with your search. A fee is charged for reproduction rights. Arrangements can be made for photographs of the materials you select.

4. Chambers of Commerce

Most fairly sizable towns have a Chamber of Commerce. Often archival materials in the form of old photographs are maintained by these organizations.

5. Historical Societies

Many towns have a historical society—a museum where important events related to the history of the town are recorded. They keep archives with old photographs of the people, the streets, and the buildings. Historical societies are excellent resources if you are designing a publication that discusses the history of your town, or if you want to show buildings, street layouts, clothing, or automobile styles from a particular era.

SOME PICTURE SOURCES IN THE UNITED STATES
Public collections:

1. Boston Public Library, Fine Arts Department

Copley Square

Boston, MA 02177

Phone: 617. 536.5400

Pictorial materials range from the 1920s to the present. Subjects include: art, history, geography, and nature in slides, art reproductions, photographs, portraits, and postcards.

2. Brooklyn Public Library, Art & Music Division

Grand Army Plaza

Brooklyn, NY 11238

Phone: 718. 636.3214

Pictorial materials range from prehistory to the present. Subjects include: works of art, portraits, natural history, United States history and geography, daily life, people, costumes, and more in the form of clippings, photographs, and advertisements.

3. Buffalo and Erie County Public Library, Picture Collection

Lafayette Square

Buffalo, NY 14203

Phone: 716. 856.7525

Pictorial materials range from prehistory to the present. Subjects include: portraits, history, science, literature, sports, geography in art reproductions, photographs, magazines, and books.

4. Free Library of Philadelphia, Print and Picture Department

Logan Square

Philadelphia, PA 19103

Phone: 215. 686.5405

Pictorial materials range from the 15th century to the present. Subjects include: Philadelphia history, portraits, American history, drawing and prints by American artists, old Valentine and Christmas greeting cards, cards from Philadelphia tradesmen in the form of fine arts prints, drawings, clippings, postcards, posters, stereograms, cartoons, trade cards, advertisements, and more.

5. Free Library of Philadelphia, Rare Book and Print Department

The Free Library of Philadelphia also has a rare book and print collection that includes pictorial materials from old books and prints. Subjects are: law-related old prints, history of printing, illustrations from early children's books, oriental miniatures, and medieval manuscripts.

6. Library of Congress, Prints and Photographs Division

1st Street between East Capitol & Independence
Avenue S.E.
Washington, D.C. 20540
Phone: 202. 426.6394

The Library of Congress offers a wide range of pictorial materials on general subjects from the 15th century to the present and has a catalog of images to make research easier.

7. Museum of the City of New York, Print Department

Fifth Avenue at 103rd Street
New York, NY 10029
Phone: 212. 534.4126

This museum has a collection of historical materials from the early 17th century to the present with an emphasis on New York City history.

8. New York Public Library, Picture Collection

Fifth Avenue & 42nd Street
New York, NY 10018
Phone: 212. 790.6101

The New York Public Library offers a wide variety of pictorial materials from prehistory to the present and has a catalog of their images for easy researching.

There are many more public sources for those unique and special pictures to illustrate your publications. This is just a partial listing of some of the larger collections. Many local libraries will have the image you need.

Private collections:

Private picture collections index their pictorial information by subject and charge a fee that often includes the cost of a professional search and reproduction rights. They will give you photographs of materials you want. If you do not have the time to go through many books and have the budget, this is a good way to get the pictures you need. Some of the fees for one-time use of images are quite steep. Many collections are available on CD-ROM. Some have cataloged images that can be viewed on the World Wide Web.

An assortment of private collections are listed below.

1. Archive Photos

530 West 25th Street
New York, NY 10001
Phone: 212. 675.0115

Founded in 1990 Archive Photos is a significant source of historical images. Their library of images covers all subjects from early civilization to the present and includes American and world history, sports, politics, current events, and the arts.

2. Bettmann

902 Broadway
New York, NY 10010
Phone: 212. 777.6200

This is a well-known source with over 17 million pictorial items that include color and black-and-white photographs, engravings, and woodcuts of interest to designers on all subjects from prehistory to the present. They maintain a catalog that lists all their holdings. Microsoft has purchased the entire Bettmann archive and will be putting all the images into a digital format available on CD-ROM.

3. Comstock

30 Irving Place
New York, NY 10003
Phone: 800. 225.2727
E-mail: service@comstock.com

Comstock offers over five million images of digitized photographic images for designers. Images are available on CD-ROM and its on-line services, and include: people scenes, sports, travel, industrial, wildlife, and many others.

4. Corbis Media

15395 SE 30th Place, Suite 300

Bellevue, WA 98007

Phone: 800. 260.0444

E-mail: cmedia@corbis.com

Web site: http://www.corbis.com

Corbis Media has a large collection of fine arts images that are available for licensing to designers. They offer a wide array of technology and service options. Images can be sampled on their web site.

5. Corel Corporation

1600 Carling Avenue

Ottawa, Ontario, K1Z 8R7

Canada

Phone: 800. 772.6735

Corel Corporation is a developer and marketer of computer graphics for designers and desktop publishers. Their Professional Photos Library consists of 200 CD-ROM titles with 20,000 photos. The CD-ROMs are sold separately or as a package, and the photographs are available royalty-free.

6. Digital Stock Corporation

400 South Sierra Avenue, Suite 100

Solana Beach, CA 92705

Phone: 800. 545.4515

Digital Stock is a publisher of high-quality stock photographs on CD-ROM. Its catalog, Catalog Disk 2.0, with preview images, is available for a nominal fee.

7. The Stock Market

360 Park Avenue South

New York, NY 10010

Phone: 800. 999.0800

The Stock Market has a library of two million contemporary images of people, sports, transportation, food, science, and communication and represents over 250 photographers.

There are many more private collections. Consult your library.

Books as picture sources:

1. *Picture Sources: Collections of Prints and Photographs in the U.S.A. and Canada*
   Special Libraries Association, NY
   This book is a good resource—one that is used by professional and nonprofessional picture researchers. It lists public and private picture sources geographically and according to subject matter.

2. *The Art Director's Black Book*
   This book maintains of list of sources for all kinds of illustrative materials for art directors and graphic designers, including drawings and photographs.

3. *A Descriptive Analysis of the Library of Congress Paper Print Collection and Related Copyright Materials*
   By Patrick Loughney
   U.M.I., Ann Arbor, MI 48106

4. *Picture Researcher's Handbook: an International Guide to Picture Sources and How to Use Them. (1992)*
   By Hilary Evans
   Van Nostrand Reinhold, London: Blueprint; New York

6. *The Complete Encyclopedia of Illustration (1979)*
   By J. G. Heck
   Park Lane, New York, NY
   This book contains 11,725 copyright-free engravings from the 19th century.

7. *Bettmann Portable Archive*
   Bettmann Department GD1
   902 Broadway
   New York, NY 10010
   Phone: 800. 897.3377

The Bettmann Portable Archive contains over 6,000 images in color and black-and-white—a handy book to help locate that special image.

COPYRIGHT BASICS

When selecting illustrations for your publication, it is essential to be aware of any possible legal difficulties that may arise. There are three legal aspects that should concern you:

1. Ownership of work

In 1976, the Copyright Act was revised to give artists and authors more rights to ownership than they had in the preceding years. If you hire an illustrator or photographer, that person, according to the law, owns the copyright and is giving you a one-time right to use it. The only time this is not the case is:

- when the creator of the work signs over all rights to the work
- if the creator of the work is a staff member of your organization and not a freelancer

2. Defamation of reputation

If you use a photograph in a publication that you design showing people or a person in a damaging way or false light, it is considered defamatory and you can be held liable.

3. Commercial use beyond your publication

If you use a photograph in your publication that another designer or advertising agency wants to use, you must get a signed release from the model or person in that photograph or photographs.

 It is always a good idea to make sure you are covered legally when using any illustration. Find out your rights. Familiarize yourself with the copyright laws.

Top right: Cover and inside page from the Spring 1988 issue of *Currents*, the quarterly newsletter of Hobart and William Smith Colleges that is sent to prospective students. Clip art from Dover Publications was used in the original publication shown here. Subsequent issues use photographs in combination with clip art images to create a more contemporary look, and to appeal to the teen-age audience.
Designers: Elizabeth Clark, Gwen Butler
Art director: Bernice Thieblot
Publications Editor: Pat Blakeslee

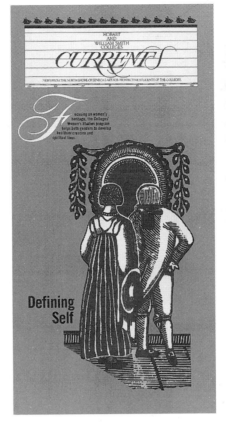

Below: Inside pages of the Astronomy Bulletin for Brigham Young University. The astronomy-related images were donations from alumni for the university's unique collection.
Designer: McRay Magelby

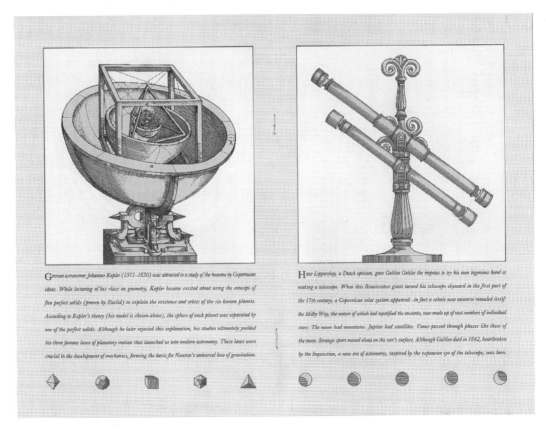

How did she do that?

A list of the graphic devices used in this chapter and how each was created

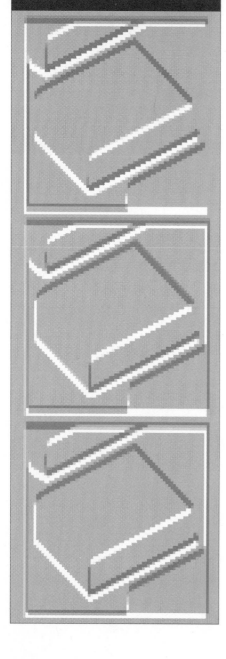

1. The number seven was created from the font called Ann-Stone. It was converted to paths in FreeHand where the black lines were changed to white and filled with a gradual fill.

2. This drop cap was treated the same way as the number seven.

3. The book graphic is clip art from T/Maker and is used as a bullet to identify the public library collections. The column on the left was created in Photoshop using this book graphic and the embossing filter.

4. This bullet is from the font called Type Embellishments Two from Fontek.

Appendix 1
Sampler
of Digital Clip Art

Appendix 1
Sampler of Digital Clip Art

"In art, quantity is meaningless: it's quality that counts.
Period. The right image is a treasure: finding it
will lift your project beyond your imagination."

—John McWade, *Before & After*, Vol. 4 No. 4, 1995.

ou need some drawings for your publication but you can't draw or don't have the time to render an appropriate drawing. Your budget will not permit you to hire an illustrator. What are your options? The answer is clip art—ready-made, instant art— art available on disk, CD-ROM, or in books.

Ready-made art used as spot illustrations can be effective and save money and time for the designer and the client. Most of the available clip art can be altered to suit your publication.

Manufacturers of digital images are producing art in many drawing styles and numerous categories—business, people, media, medicine and health, maps—you name it. There is clip art of textures that can be used to create an interesting background or ambience for a page—a way to spiff up an otherwise dull layout, and clip art with generic stock photographs. Some clip art is royalty- and copyright-free. Some require a usage fee.

The following pages showcase a small sampling of available images from a few of the many software manufacturers of clip art and stock images. Each producer of clip art represented here has many more images in many different styles and colors. Some of these images have been altered to reduce memory.

QUESTIONS TO ASK BEFORE PURCHASING CLIP ART

How can you be sure you are getting the clip art package(s) that will best suit your needs? The following questions may help you make a decision.

1. **Will the clip art you are considering run on your computer?**

2. **Do the images have the right feel for the kind of printed pieces or presentations you create?**

3. **Does the package you are considering have enough themes for repeated use?**

4. **Will the images take up a great deal of your computer's memory causing your computer to crash?**

   Some of the background textures and photographic images take up huge amounts of memory. Make sure you know how much memory will be consumed by the images you are considering.

5. **Does the artwork look professional? Will it reproduce well without jagged edges?**

   Clip art packages are available at different prices. Some of them are quite inexpensive, but the art looks amateurish and does not print out well. Make sure the collection you are interested in has a catalog so you can view the images in printed form.

6. **Do you want your clip art on disks or CD-ROMs?**

   Digital clip art comes either on floppy disks or CD-Rom. If your computer has a CD-ROM port, get your clip art on CD-ROM. It is easier to store.

Take your time before purchasing clip art collections. Send for catalogs from different software manufacturers to see what is available before making a decision. Some clip art or stock art companies charge by the image. Make sure you know what you are getting before you make your purchase.

PO Box 709
Murtle Creek, OR 94457
Phone: 800. 444.9392
Fax: 541. 863.4547

Artbeats has a large assortment
of images that can be used as
background textures for printed
materials and multimedia
presentations. The resolution
has been reduced on the images
on this page.

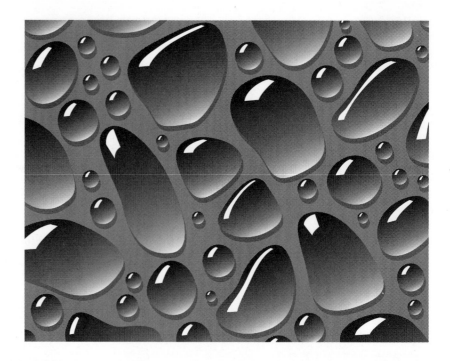

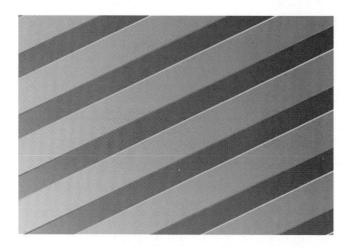

Aztech New Media Corporation

1 Scarsdale Road
Don Mills, Ontario
Canada M3B 2R2
Phone: 416. 449.4787
Fax: 416. 449.1058

Aztech New Media Corporation has a large collection of high and low resolution photographic stock images and line art images on CD-ROM in many different categories, such as agriculture, anatomy, animals, architecture, borders and backgrounds, business, cartoons, communications, computers, education, nature, people, views from space, and numerous others.

Cartesia Map Art

5 South Main Street, Box 757
Lambertville, NJ 08530
Phone: 800. 334.4291
Fax: 609. 397.5724

Cartesia makes maps for
graphic designers that can be
edited in a drawing program,
such as FreeHand, CorelDraw,
or Illustrator. World maps, major
countries, states, provinces, and
continents, are included on their
CD-ROMs.

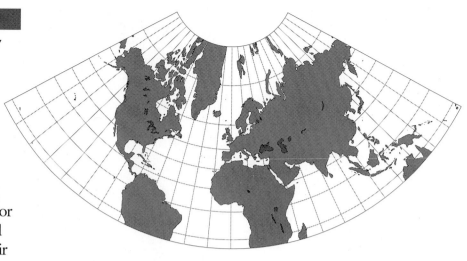

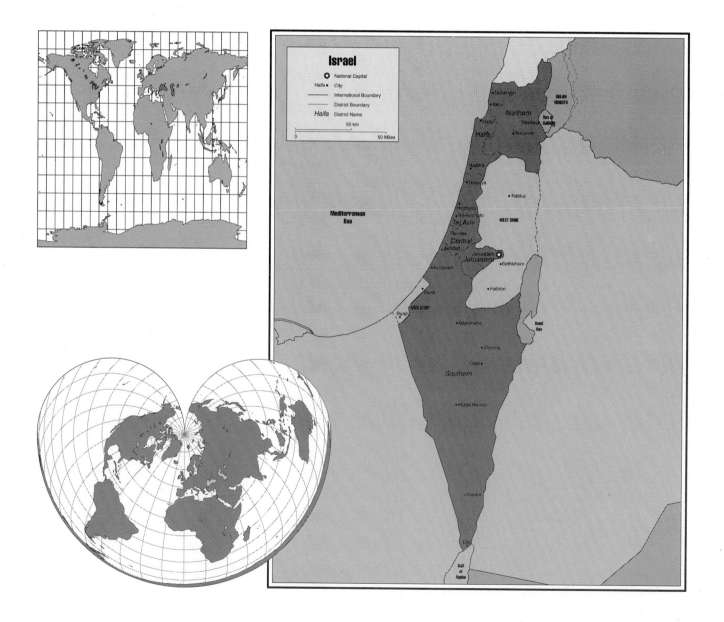

Corel Corporation

1600 Carling Avenue
Ottawa, Ontario,
Canada K1Z 8R7
Phone: 800. 772.6735
Fax: 613. 728.2891

Corel Gallery is a library of over 10,000 clip art images. Corel has CD-ROMs with a large selection of ready-to-use photographic stock images in numerous categories.

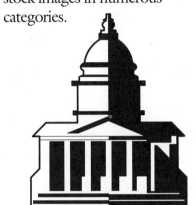

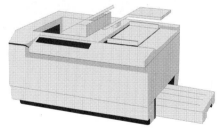

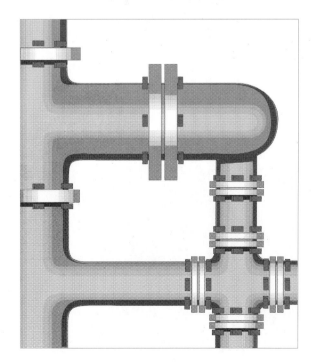

400 South Sierra Avenue, Suite 100
Salana Beach, CA 92075
Phone: 800. 545.4514
Fax: 619. 794.4041

Digital Stock provides stock
photography on CD-ROMs.
The generic images can be
altered in image-editing
programs, such as Photoshop,
Picture Publisher, or Photostyler.
The library of images include
animals, textures, transportation,
business and industry, and
numerous others.

Dynamic Graphics, Inc.

6000 North Forest Park Drive
PO Box 1901
Peoria, IL 61656-9941
Phone: 800. 255.8800
Fax: 309. 688.5873

Dynamic Graphics produces digital clip art images in three different series—Electronic Clipper, Designer Club Series, and Electronic Print Media—with a large assortment of categories. The images on this page represent a small sampling of their offerings.

Seymour Chwast Collection
5 East 19th Street
New York, NY 10003
Phone: 800. 898.8461
Fax: 212. 475.4429

The drawings in the Flat File
Edition CD-ROMs have been
created by Seymour Chwast,
a well-known illustrator and
designer. There are five volumes
in this collection. Each volume
deals with a different category
(1. People, 2. Business, Politics
and Education, 3. Animals,
4. Food, Home, & Leisure,
5. Places and Things).

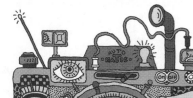

Harter Image Archives

4139 Gardendale, Suite 207
San Antonio, TX
Phone: 210. 614.5942
Fax: 210. 614.5922

Harter Image Archives has a large selection of assorted antique images in CD-ROM format. These images, 19th and 20th century wood engravings, were collected by Jim Harter, editor of eleven clip art books for Dover Publications and Bonanza Books. These images are arranged in categories—art supplies, banking, birds, frames, globes, insects, mythological animals, trunks and chests, and numerous others.

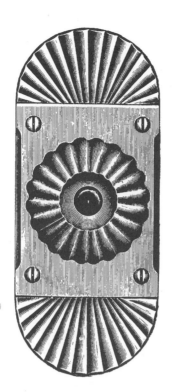

Dan Pelavin Illustrations
80 Varick Street Suite 3B
New York, NY 10013-1925
Phone: 212. 941.7418
Fax: 212. 431.7138

Illustrated Stock Cuts for Art Directors and Designers, 3rd Edition, is a catalog of over 1000 images that are available in digital format and created by illustrator Daniel Pelavin whose work has appeared in many books and magazines. The images in many different categories are available for reproduction for a fee. Fees are based upon usage. The images are copyrighted original material and may not be reproduced without permission.

Image Club Graphics

10545 West Donges Court
Milwaukee, WI 53224-9985
Phone: 800. 661.9410
Fax: 403. 261.7013

Image Club Graphics offers a wide variety of clip art that includes fonts, background patterns, borders, and images from different countries. Their images come in different styles and include sketchy line drawings, silhouettes, and woodcuts.

Metro Creative Graphics, Inc.

33 West 34 Street
New York, NY 10001
Phone: 212.947.5100
Fax: 212.714.9139

Metro Creative Graphics has been a resource of graphic images for artists and designers for over 85 years. A large and comprehensive art and idea service, Metro Creative Graphics offers clip art as Laser Art CD-ROM or traditional print. The service is subscription only.

Past-Tints Antique Illustrations
7475 Brydon Road
LaVerne, CA 91750
Phone: 800. 593.3556
Fax: 909. 593.6062

Past-Tints is a collection of
digitized antique illustrations that
date back to the late 19th century.
Some of the categories of images
include people, animals, illustrated
capital letters, and transportation.

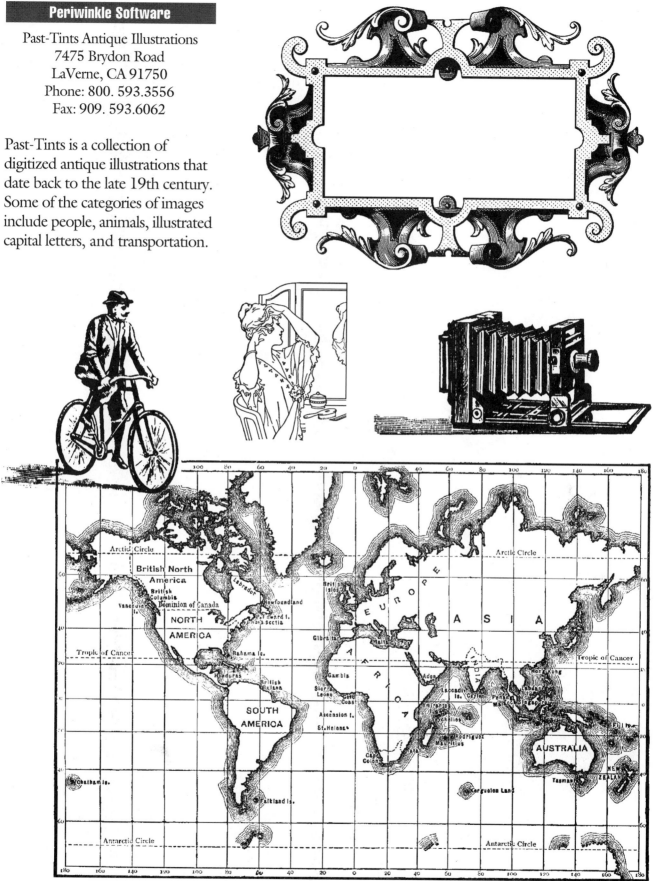

T/Maker Company

1390 Villa Street
Mountain View, CA 94041
Phone: 415. 962.0195
Fax: 415. 962.0201

T/Maker has a large assortment of images for reproduction in different categories, styles, and colors.

Ultimate Symbol Inc.

31 Wilderness Drive
Stony Point, NY 10980-3447
Phone: 914. 942.0003
Fax: 914. 942.0004

Ultimate Symbol is a collection of digital stock symbols in CD-ROM format that were created, collected, and compiled over a period of 50 years. The images are organized according to category: Zodiac, typographic devices, printer's ornaments, arrows, and numerous others.

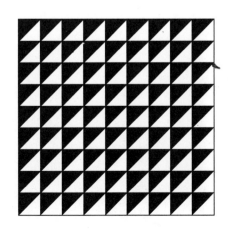

How did she do that?

A list of the graphic devices used in this chapter and how each was created

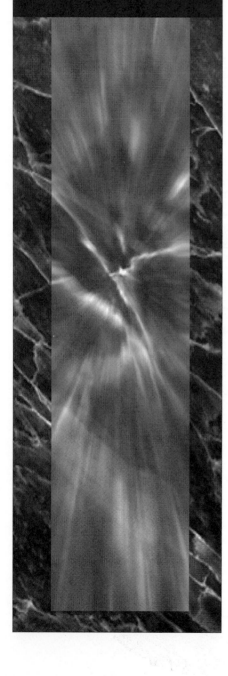

1.

This CD-ROM is clip art from T/Maker.

2.

This drop cap that appears on the first page of this chapter is from the Fontek font called Old Dreadful. It was converted to paths in FreeHand and filled with a graduated fill.

3.

The hand with the disk is from the font called DF Industrials Two from Fontek.

4.

The marble in the column on the left is clip art from Artbeats. It was brought into Photoshop. The middle portion was selected with the marquee tool, and the radial blur filter was applied.

Appendix 2
Sampler
of Specialty Fonts

Sampler of Specialty Fonts

"The word 'font' as in type font, has been altered in meaning to the point where it no longer refers to letterforms but to a computer code. In digital terms, fonts are moving pictures and collections of shapes."

—Darcy DiNucci, *Print* magazine. May/June 1995.

 onts are available in different varieties and styles. Some are strictly pictorial, without letters, symbols, or numbers. Since these are graphic images, and are installed in your computer's system like other fonts, they provide ready-made, instant art that can be easily used as illustrations.

There are specialty fonts—fonts that are decorative, fonts that are playful or funky. Some fonts should only be used in small amounts of text because they are not very readable if used in a large body of text. These should be used as headlines, or in sentences with very few words. These specialty fonts can help dress up any publication and attract attention if used properly.

The fonts you select for your publication should enhance the overall message you are trying to get across. Many specialty fonts are playful and fun to use but call attention to themselves rather than to your publication. If the font(s) you use for your publication is difficult to read, it will not be read. Specialty fonts should be thought of as a delicacy—good in small amounts, overwhelming when overused.

The following pages provide a small sampling of the numerous fonts that are available.

Glossary
of Terminology

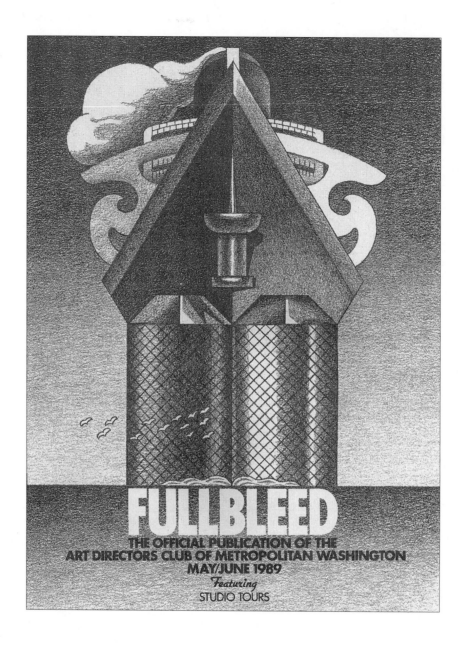

Cover for *Fullbleed*, the official publication of The Art Director's Club of Metropolitan Washington.
The issue featured "Studio Tours" and the illustration, rendered in pencil
was a take-off on the famous Cassandre travel poster.
Illustrator: David R. Street
Designer: Miu Eng

Glossary
of Terminology

Ampersand

The symbol for the word "and" (&). Each font has an ampersand unique to that typeface.

Anti-aliasing

The anti-alias feature smooths edges created with painting, type, or selection tools.

Auto exposure

A feature found in scanning programs that makes automatic adjustments in the brightness and contrast of an image.

Bar chart

A chart format that shows statistical information by comparing items with bars or columns of different lengths or heights.

Baud

The rate of speed of a modem measured in bits per second.

Bit-mapped image

Type or graphics from paint programs formed by a series of dots and are jagged in appearance.

Bleed

An illustration or inked area that runs off the edge of a page.

Blueline or brownline

A proof in blue or brown prepared by the printer as a final check for the designer to catch mistakes before a job goes to press.

Brightness

A term that describes the differences in the intensity of reflected light on an image. It is one of the dimensions of color.

Bullet

A typographic element for listing items in a publication. The bullet provides graphic interest on a page.

Camera-ready art

The completed design including all art, photographs, and text ready for reproduction by a printer.

Caption

Information about a photograph or other image that identifies it. Also called a cutline.

CD-ROM

A system of storing large amounts of information on a compact disc for retrieval on the computer.

Clip art

Line art or photographs found in books or on disk to be used in a page design. Most clip art is uncopyrighted art—art that can be used without permission.

Clipboard

The place where the computer stores text, or a graphic that is cut or copied from a document to be pasted into another place. The clipboard gets erased when the computer is shut down.

CMYK

Cyan, magenta, yellow, and black—process colors.

Collage

A composite of different materials combined to form one picture. It is possible to create collages in image-editing programs by putting paintings, drawings, and photographs together.

Color separations

Negatives for printing the four primary subtractive colors—cyan, magenta, yellow, and black.

Computer graphics

Graphics or designs created on a computer.

Contact sheet

Sheet of photographs showing many frames from a roll of film. The contact sheet is used to proof photographs before enlarging.

Continued line

A line of text at the bottom of an article to indicate the page where the article is continued.

Continuous tone art

Photographs or detailed line art with a wide range of gray tones from black to white.

Contrast

A tonal range from black to white or dark colors to lighter ones in photographs and type.

Cool colors

Colors that are associated with the natural world (blues and greens).

Crop marks

Lines on the camera-ready art that indicate where the page is to be trimmed.

Cropping

The process of eliminating extraneous elements in a photograph to make the image more powerful, and a way to change the proportions of a picture.

Cropping "L's"

Two right angles to help determine where a photograph should be cropped.

Cutline

Information about a photograph or other image that identifies it. Also called a caption.

Decisive moment

This is the exact moment in photography where the photographer captures a memorable shot that would have been lost if taken later.

Demographic information

Specific data with information on reaching an audience. Helpful information for marketing a product to a particular group of people.

Die cut

A see through or cutout in a piece of paper that is made by a die removing a portion of the paper in a specific outline shape.

Digital halftone

A photograph or continuous tone art that has been scanned and turned in into a series of dots (gray scale) and is ready for printing.

Dingbat

A decorative element, or graphic device for listing items, or to provide decoration on a page.

Display type

Large type, often bold, that is used in headlines to grab attention.

Dodging

Lightening a particular area in a photograph to improve the quality and contrast.

Dots per inch (dpi)

The measurement that refers to resolution, sharpness, or clarity of a printer, a computer monitor, or an output.

Download

To transfer information from one computer or other electronic device (modem or fax) to another.

Drop cap

A large initial capital letter dropped into the beginning of a paragraph to add visual interest on a page.

Dummy

A sketch of an idea for a page layout used as an aid in working out the full page design. The piece given to a printer as a guide for the final publication.

Duotone

Rich one-color photograph produced by printing a halftone negative using one color on top of a tinted screen in another color.

Emboss

A filter in an image-editing program that gives the impression of being raised above the surface of a piece of paper.

Encapsulated PostScript (EPS)

A format used in graphics programs to smooth out graphics so there are no jagged edges. The files can be resized in a page layout program.

Extended type

Type with characters wider than normal, an effect that can be achieved in a page layout program.

Foil stamping

An operation in printing where a metallic strip or foil is laminated onto paper.

For position only (fpo)

A photocopied or scanned photograph, or other art placed on a page to indicate where the actual art should be placed after it has been screened.

Four-color process printing

The process of printing color that combines cyan, magenta, yellow, and black to reproduce all colors of the spectrum.

Freelancer

A self-employed person not tied to an employer.

Front-end

The technology (hardware and software) used at the beginning of the production process.

Graduated fill

A screened fill for an object with tones from light to dark, or from dark to light that is available in most drawing and image-editing programs.

Halftone

In order for a photograph or other continuous tone art to be reproduced, a screen is used to break up the image into different dots. This can be achieved on a scanner.

High-end technology

High resolution electronic technology, sophisticated and precise (e.g., Linotronic).

Hue

The name of a color.

Icon

A small graphic or symbol used for identification.

Imagesetter

Typesetting machine found in service bureaus and used for high-resolution output.

Inline graphic

A graphic inserted into a line of text that becomes imbedded in the text. When the text block is moved, the graphic moves along with it.

Jumpline

A line of text at the bottom of an article to indicate the page where the article is continued.

Linear fill

A fill that goes in a straight line from one point to another.

Line art

A drawing composed of lines. The opposite of continous tone art.

Line screen

The shape, angle, and density of halftone dots.

Lines per inch (lpi)

A way of measuring resolution.

Linotronic

A high-resolution imagesetter or PostScript printer. Resolution runs from 1200 dots per inch to over 5000.

Logotype

A logo for an organization composed of all type.

Magenta

One of the four colors used in a full-color printing process (purple-red).

Megabyte (MB)

One million bytes of information.

Midtones

The gray level of an image between 25 percent and 75 percent. Image editing programs give you the ability to adjust the midtones of a photograph.

Moiré pattern

An effect caused by rescreening a halftone.

Mortise

A part or area cut out of a halftone.

Mug shot

A close up photograph of a person in a newspaper or magazine.

Negative space

The white space or ground opposite a figure.

Noise

Pixels randomly distributed in an image.

Object-oriented graphic

A graphic created with defined mathematical lines that can be resized and maintain its integrity. The opposite of a paint (bit-map) graphic.

Output

The product of a desktop printer or imagesetter, paper or film printout.

Overlay

A sheet of acetate or paper placed over a mechanical with instructions for the printer pertaining to color, bleeds, and other pertinent information.

Page layout program

A software program for design that enables the designer to import text and graphics in order to create a publication on the computer.

PANTONE® Matching System

Color publication guides to help the designer communicate colors for reproduction.

Pasteboard

The area outside the page in a page layout program that acts as a drawing board for type or graphics that need to be moved to another page.

Photo mechanical transfer (PMT)

A positive screened print made from a piece of art ready for placement on a mechanical.

Photomontage

A collage or composite of different photographs put together to create an interesting visual.

PICT format

A format used to see graphics on a computer monitor and save them for reworking or importing into a page layout program.

Pictograph or pictogram

A pictorial representation of an object as a symbol. Originally an image drawn on a rock.

Pie chart

A chart in the shape of a pie. The statistical information is shown as parts of a whole.

Pixel

Smallest measurement on the computer that determines the clarity or resolution of an image.

PostScript

A page description language that allows the computer to communicate with a printer.

Printer font

The font stored in the system of the computer that enables the printer to recognize a typeface during printing. If the font is not in the system, the printer will select another font.

Process color

The four colors used in color printing (CMYK).

Pull quotes, breakouts, or call outs

A quotation or sentence extracted from a paragraph and used as a visual device on a page.

Radial fill

A fill in a drawing or image-editing program that goes from the center in all direction.

RAM

The random access memory inside the computer where data is stored.

Rebus

The use of pictures or symbols as a substitute for words.

Registration marks

The marks used on all pages of a document with color that enables the printer to register the color.

Reversals or drop outs

White type on a black or screened color background.

Resolution

The crispness or clarity of an image or type either on a monitor or an output device.

Runaround

Text in a page layout or drawing program that wraps around a graphic. Also referred to as text wrap.

Saturation

The purity or intensity of a color.

Sharpening

A way of increasing the sharpness and contrast in an image-editing program.

Show through

The print on the opposite side of a paper that is visible from the other side of the page and makes it difficult to read either side.

Silhouette

A technique where the background of an image is eliminated to make an image stand out.

Sizing

Reducing or enlarging an illustration or photograph to fit within a space on the page.

Spot color

The addition of an extra color in a design.

Stock agency

A business with a collection of images—clip art, or photographs—that can be rented for use by designers for specific publications.

Stripping

The method used by a printer to place screened photographs into a film to create a plate for printing.

Swash

A decorative stroke on a letter.

Swipe file

File of images or designs to stimulate ideas.

Text wrap

A line of text that is wrapped around a graphic.

Thumbnails

A preliminary sketch for the design of a page that shows placement of text and graphics.

TIFF

Tag Image File Format. A format for storing and importing images into a page layout program.

Tint

A screen that changes the percentage of a color.

Toolbox

The set of tools in a painting, drawing, or image-editing program.

Typography

The art and design of type.

Unsharp mask

A filter in an image-editing program that helps sharpen areas of a photograph or other image.

Value

The lightness, brightness, or darkness of a color.

Velox

A halftone photograph in black and white.

Vignette

A halftone that gradually fades off.

Warm colors

Red, yellow, and the blends of these colors.

Width

The horizontal measurement of a letter—condensed, normal, or expanded.

Window

A black or red box on a mechanical where a screened photograph is dropped in.

WYSIWYG

What you see is what you get (on the computer monitor or in the printout).

Index

Colophon

**(Factual information related to the production
and printing of a book that may include typefaces
and software and hardware used)**

HARDWARE:
Quadra 650
SyQuest 44/88MB
UMax UC840 scanner
Sony Triniton 17" monitor
LaserWriter II for proofs

SOFTWARE:
PageMaker 5.0
FreeHand 4.0
Photoshop 3.0

TYPEFACES:
Body text: Galliard
Headlines and subheads: Helvetica Compressed
All other typefaces are identified in each chapter